KU-682-840

Promising Practices
for Partnering with Families
in the Early Years

A volume in
Family–School–Community Partnership
Diana B. Hiatt-Michael, *Series Editor*

Promising Practices for Partnering with Families in the Early Years

Edited by

Mary M. Cornish
Plymouth State University

≡IAP

INFORMATION AGE PUBLISHING, INC.
Charlotte, NC • www.infoagepub.com

Z009003896

Library of Congress Cataloging-in-Publication Data

Promising practices for partnering with families in the early years / edited by Mary M. Cornish.
    p. cm. – (Family-school-community partnership)
 Includes bibliographical references.
 ISBN 978-1-59311-946-1 (pbk.) – ISBN 978-1-59311-947-8 (hardcover)
 I. Cornish, Mary M.
 LC225.P763 2008
 371.19'2–dc22

                                           2008022760

Copyright © 2008 Information Age Publishing Inc.

All rights reserved. No part of this publication may be reproduced, stored in a retrieval system, or transmitted, in any form or by any means, electronic, mechanical, photocopying, microfilming, recording or otherwise, without written permission from the publisher.

Printed in the United States of America

CONTENTS

ACKNOWLEDGMENTS

As editor, I would like to express my sincere appreciation to all those who have contributed to this collaborative endeavor. Special thanks go to the many outstanding national and international scholars who eagerly committed to this project. They gave generously of their time and expertise. Their substantive work has made this publication possible.

I would like to extend my deep gratitude to Diana Hiatt-Michael for giving me the opportunity to edit this volume in this prestigious series. She had confidence in me, and gave moral support throughout the process. I sincerely appreciate her mentoring.

Thanks to the Family, School, Community Partnerships Special Interest Group of the American Educational Research Association for its sponsorship of the monograph series.

Peer reviewers Lori Connor-Tadros, Diana Hiatt-Michael, Pat Hulsebosch, Ollie Moles, Virginia Shipman, and Lee Shumow are also gratefully acknowledged. Their thoughtful feedback enhanced the quality of the work presented here.

Special appreciation goes to Shannon McCurry, an undergraduate Early Childhood Studies major at Plymouth State University, who brought an invaluable perspective to the review process. She gave extensive feedback to help make the monograph accessible for preservice early childhood educators. I enjoyed discussing every chapter with Shannon and hearing her enthusiasm for applying what she learned.

I am grateful to Plymouth State University for providing me with a sabbatical to engage in this endeavor.

Thanks to Connie Kim, Jong-Yoon Kim, and Meredith Leighton for agreeing to be photographed for the cover; also to Karen Sanders for coordinating the photo shoot.

Promising Practices for Partnering with Families in the Early Years, pages vii–viii
Copyright © 2008 by Information Age Publishing
All rights of reproduction in any form reserved.

I would also like to thank my dear friend and colleague, Pat Cantor, for sharing her many thoughtful insights and support throughout this project.

I am extremely grateful to all the families with whom I have worked over the years. From them I have learned so much about partnering with families in meaningful and culturally responsive ways.

Finally, I wish to extend my deepest appreciation to my partner, John Krueckeberg. I could not have accomplished this project without his outstanding editing acumen, technical expertise, photography skills, love, and generous support.

LIST OF CONTRIBUTORS

Mary Jane Brotherson Professor, Department of Human Development and Family Studies, Iowa State University

Margaret Caspe Consultant, Harvard Family Research Project

Douglas P. Clark Associate Professor and Program Director, Early Childhood Administration. National-Louis University

Lori Connor-Tadros Vice President, Children and Family Services, The Finance Project

Carl Corter Professor and Atkinson Charitable Foundation Chair, Atkinson Centre and Institute of Child Study, Department of Human Development and Applied Psychology, Ontario Institute for Studies in Education. University of Toronto

Wm. Justin Dyer Doctoral Student, Department of Human and Community Development, University of Illinois at Urbana–Champaign

Billie J. Enz Interim Associate Dean, School of Educational Innovation and Teacher Preparation, Arizona State University at the Polytechnic Campus

Judy Harris Helm President, Consultant, and Author, Best Practices, Inc.

Brent A. McBride Professor of Human Development, Department of Human and Community Development, University of Illinois at Urbana–Champaign

Marilyn LaCount Director of Office of Youth Preparation, Arizona State University, Downtown Center

Promising Practices for Partnering with Families in the Early Years, pages ix–x
Copyright © 2008 by Information Age Publishing
All rights of reproduction in any form reserved.

ix

M. Elena Lopez   Senior Consultant, Harvard Family Research Project

Sejal Patel   Doctoral Candidate, Atkinson Centre and Institute of Child Study, Department of Human Development and Applied Psychology, Ontario Institute for Studies in Education, University of Toronto

Janette Pelletier   Associate Professor, Atkinson Centre and Institute of Child Study, Department of Human Development and Applied Psychology, Ontario Institute for Studies in Education, University of Toronto

Dawn Ramsburg   Child Care Program Specialist, Childcare Bureau

Thomas R. Rane   Associate Professor, Department of Home and Family, Brigham Young University–Idaho

Michelle Rhodes   Director of Leaps and Bounds, Office of Youth Preparation, Arizona State University

Jean Ann Summers   Research Professor, Beach Center on Disability, University of Kansas

Heather Weiss   Founder and Director, Harvard Family Research Project

Pamela J. Winton   Senior Scientist and Director of Outreach, Frank Porter Graham Child Development Institute; Research Professor, School of Education, University of North Carolina–Chapel Hill

FOREWORD

Diana B. Hiatt-Michael
Series Editor,
Family–School–Community Partnership Series

Welcome to the sixth monograph in the Family–School–Community Partnership Series. This series of monographs has been edited and developed by members of the American Educational Research Association's (AERA) Special Interest Group–Family, School, Community Partnerships (SIG-FSCP). This volume is directed toward research to practice issues related to partnering with families of children birth through age 5.

The critical importance of parents, parenting, and a child's development and learning during the early years has been significantly researched and documented during the past century. This research undergirds current efforts that partner parents and families with formal and informal early educational programs for their children. Early childhood education has assumed renewed national interest since recent research on the development of the brain has supported the importance of cognitive development in the early years. Thus, states across the country are considering legislation for universal pre school. At the federal level, Head Start and related programs received recent reauthorization; whereas, K–12 legislation remains in committee debates. Presidential candidates include support for early education on their platforms.

Mary M. Cornish, Associate Professor of Early Childhood Studies at Plymouth State University, accepted the SIG-FSCP invitation to serve as Editor for this particular monograph. Cornish, who has been active in the early childhood field for over 25 years, is highly regarded for her research on family involvement, including Smart Start, a nationally acclaimed early childhood initiative. She has received numerous awards, in particular the

Promising Practices for Partnering with Families in the Early Years, pages xi–xii
Copyright © 2008 by Information Age Publishing
All rights of reproduction in any form reserved. **xi**

American Educational Research Association's SIG-FSCP's Outstanding Dissertation Award in 2000 for *Patriarchs, Pawns, and Pluralists: Parent and Business Participation in Three North Carolina Early Childhood Reform Partnerships* (Doctoral dissertation, University of North Carolina, Chapel Hill, 1999).

Cornish served as Chair of the SIG-FSCP from 2003 to 2005. Throughout this period she supported both my work as editor of this series and the selected authors' contributions. She organized individuals to serve as a review board for the thrust of each monograph, topics of chapters, and reviewers for the chapters. During this period, Cornish was acquiring the knowledge and skills to assume the role of editor. Thus, I knew that this volume was in kind and skilled hands. My deepest appreciation goes to her for her care and nurturing of the authors and chapters that comprise this timely and important monograph.

At the SIG's buisiness meeting in AERA at the start of the new millennium, members expressed concern that, although sufficient research in promising practices for parent involvement in schools had been amassed, the field lacked a method to disseminate that research. This series of monographs was born during that business meeting.

The initial monograph of the series, *Promising Practices for Family Involvement in Schools*, synthesized research and practice across the generic elements of family involvement in schooling. However, an idea does not materialize and become self-sustaining without the support of many key players. George Johnson and IAP have played a pivotal publication role in making sure that our idea became a reality and would be sustained.

Thus, this first monograph was followed by monographs that addressed various types of family involvement concerns, such as community involvement in *Promising Practices to Connect Schools with the Community*, families of children with special needs in *Promising Practices Connecting Schools to Families of Children with Special Needs*, global concerns in *Promising Practices for Family Involvement Across the Continents*, and families of English language learners in *Promising Practices for Teachers to Engage Families of English Language Learners*. In these monographs we noted that a major body of research attended to elementary school issues.

This monograph is fulfilling an important rold in the FSCP series. This sixth volume analyzes family involvement practices across a variety of settings and programs at the early childhood level. The initial chapters in this monograph review recent research on the importance of family involvement during the child's early years. Following chapters address significant issues, such as the role of fathers in a young child's education, home-based care, special services for parents of young children, transition programs, and the community school. Outstanding authors were invited to contribute chapters on their areas of expertise.

INTRODUCTION

Mary M. Cornish

Research shows that there are clear connections between early childhood experiences and children's development and learning. It also reveals that high-quality environments, qualified personnel, and family engagement are all critical factors in enhancing young children's early learning experiences and their subsequent educational outcomes (Cost, Quality, and Outcomes Study Team,1995; National Institute of Child Health and Human Development Early Child Care Research Network, 2000). This monograph focuses on one essential aspect of optimizing young children's development and academic success: partnering with the families of children from birth through age 5.

Partnering differs from traditional views of parent involvement. Families are not solely recipients of services and their participation is much more than simply carrying out the goals and practices of early childhood programs. In a partnership, participants are equals who share power, engage in two-way communication, and collaborate on behalf of young children. All partners, including the family, bring valued strengths and skills to the relationship (Gonzale-Mena, 2007). Partnering with families involves respecting their languages, preferences, and aspirations as well as acknowledging families as "the primary decision maker[s] in all efforts to provide family-focused, culturally consistent services" (Regional Educational Laboratories' Early Childhood Collaboration Network, 2002, p. 15).

The early childhood field has a long-standing tradition of, and a strong commitment to, working with families. This commitment is influenced by the belief that parents are a child's first and most significant teacher and

Promising Practices for Partnering with Families in the Early Years, pages xiii–xvii
Copyright © 2008 by Information Age Publishing
All rights of reproduction in any form reserved.

that families are of primary importance in promoting children's development (National Association for the Education of Young Children, 2005).
Over the last several decades, establishing partnerships with families within
their community contexts has emerged as the predominant approach for
engaging families (National Institute on Early Childhood Development
and Education [NIECDE], 2001). Two factors especially have contributed
to placing an increasing value upon this promising practice. One is a broad
societal trend toward realigning the balance of power families hold in relation to professionals and social institutions. Another is the increasing
frequency with which early childhood professionals are serving ever-more
diverse families who have cultural, ethnic, and linguistic differences from
their own (NIECDE, 2001).

Collectively, the chapters in this monograph assist in promoting and
strengthening partnerships between diverse families and those who care
for, educate, and provide support services to young children, birth through
age 5, and their families across a variety of settings. Such settings include,
but are not limited to preschool, Head Start, Early Head Start, early intervention, special education services, public PreK, kindergarten, family support programs, home-based child care, comprehensive integrated
school-based programs, and community-based programs. The chapters also
address, to varying degrees, five themes based on the principles of family-
centered partnerships:

1. Recognizing and respecting one another's knowledge and expertise;
2. Sharing information through two-way communication;
3. Sharing power and decision making;
4. Acknowledging and respecting diversity; and
5. Creating networks of support (Keyser, 2006, pp. 8–10).

The monograph supports the accomplishment of these goals as a whole
by providing important insights about exemplary programs and promising practices, informed by current research. Also, it highlights policies and
theoretical perspectives relevant to these aims.

Individual chapters offer a variety of practical strategies and recommendations that families, early childhood practitioners, policymakers, and researchers can use to enhance their knowledge and strengthen their skills for
partnering effectively. These practices are evidence-based; in other words,
research proves their effectiveness and relates to positive child, parent, and
family outcomes (Center for Evidence-Based Practices, n.d.). Additionally,
the recommended practices align with many of the exemplary practices
promoted by the National Association for the Education of Young Children
(NAEYC) and the Division for Early Childhood of the Council for Exceptional Children (DEC/CEC) in their personnel preparation guidelines.

Chapter 1 presents substantial empirical evidence about the benefits of partnering with families. It reviews recent research on family involvement processes that are related to positive outcomes for young children and highlights four family involvement program models shown to have positively impacted young children's development. The authors describe three necessary family involvement processes that are critical in supporting and promoting young children's socioemotional and cognitive growth and school readiness: *parenting, home–program relationships,* and *responsibility for learning outcomes.* They maintain these processes can, and must, be strengthened. The authors conclude with considerations for early childhood practitioners as they strive to advance all of these family involvement processes.

Chapter 2 draws upon research, primarily from early intervention/early childhood special education, to describe exemplary practices that can be used to build meaningful family–professional partnerships with all families. It describes ecological, ecocultural, and family systems theories and the ways in which theoretical knowledge of the ecology and family systems leads to establishing successful partnerships with diverse families. Additionally, it presents three broad practices and related strategies associated with effective family–professional partnerships and positive family outcomes. These include relational practices, participatory practices, and practices promoting collaboration across multiple agencies and disciplines.

Chapter 3 highlights the many benefits of partnering with fathers/males for young children, families, early childhood programs, and the larger community. The authors explain how Epstein's life-course perspective of home–school partnerships can provide an effective tool for identifying factors that may limit and/or discourage father involvement. Additionally, they confront common myths and misconceptions early childhood teachers need to overcome. The chapter depicts the promising results of a father/male involvement intervention program implemented in a large, state-funded prekindergarten (PreK) "at-risk" program. Drawing on findings and insights gained from the intervention study, the authors present 12 recommendations for successfully planning and implementing father/male involvement initiatives.

Chapter 4 examines programs that support families in providing experiences that will help prepare children for kindergarten and ensure smooth home–school transitions. The authors delineate three categories of programs: Family Support Programs, Family Interactive Programs, and Traditional Parent Education Programs. They present the common features of each category and describe eight exemplary programs representing efforts at the national, state, and local levels. Highlighting the positive outcomes for families and children's early school success, they make recommendations based on proven successes. They conclude with a brief examination of the importance of the "system-ready" concept and receptive systems in providing high-quality family support programs.

Chapter 5 explores a relatively unexamined area of family–community partnerships: family, friend, and neighbor care. The authors provide an overview of the various types of home-based care arrangements and explain the prevalence of home-based care. They explain family and child characteristics linked to home-based care and the reasons families choose it. They discuss federal and state policy efforts aimed at improving child care quality, identifying five statewide systemic initiatives and two community-based approaches that include all types of early childhood practitioners. After explaining how these efforts integrate goals related to family and community involvement in home-based care settings, the chapter concludes with a discussion of the implications for practice and promising directions for much-needed research.

Chapter 6 describes the benefits of taking diverse families' goals (for both themselves and their children) into account when they enter early childhood services. It emphasizes the necessity and benefits of seeking families' ongoing input for determining program design and delivery. The authors offer multiple strategies for determining families' goals and needs, and for ensuring that all families have a "real voice" in the process. They advocate for a knowledge-building approach to practice in which teams of professionals communicate in systematic ways to make specific improvements for partnering with families and to build better practice. Service integration is presented as a promising organizational strategy "for amplifying families' voices and engagement." The chapter depicts how all of these strategies worked in one school-based, early childhood integrated service initiative. It concludes with key findings that early childhood professionals and organizations should use to effectively pursue families' input.

Chapter 7 is the final chapter. It describes how a comprehensive, state-of-the-art community early childhood center was established in 1993 to deliver family-centered early childhood services within a community school and how it exists today. The authors highlight developments in national awareness and public policy that have precipitated important changes in the community school and influenced the model for two new schools. Expanding on one facet of the community center, a family, friend, and neighbor child care resource center, they depict how it will enhance families' and providers' access to high-quality information, resources, and technical assistance. They conclude with observations about how the new school model is "truly breaking new ground."

The *appendix* contains annotated, chapter-related recommended resources such as publications, professional organizations, and websites that should be valuable for partnering with families.

All associated with this monograph hope that readers are committed to partnering with families and are inspired to do so. We encourage you to implement the promising practices presented here, examine their impact, and seek to continually improve upon them as you engage in this important work with young children, families, and other professionals.

REFERENCES

Center for Evidence Based Practices. (n.d.). *Goals.* Retrieved October 12, 2007, from http://www.evidencebasedpractices.org/goals.php

Cost, Quality, and Outcomes Study Team. (1995). *Cost, quality, and child outcomes in child care centers, Technical report.* Denver, CO: University of Denver.

Gonzalez-Mena, J. (2007). *50 early childhood strategies for working and communicating with diverse families.* Upper Saddle River, NJ: Pearson Merrill Prentice Hall.

Keyser, J. (2006). *From parents to partners: Building a* family-centered early childhood program. St. Paul, MN: Redleaf Press.

National Association for the Education of Young Children. (2005). *Code of ethical conduct and statement of commitment.* Retrieved October 15, 2007, from http://www.naeyc.org/about/positions/PSETHOS.asp

National Institute of Child Health and Human Development Early Child Care Research Network. (2000). The relation of child care to cognitive and language development. *Child Development, 71*(4), 960–980.

National Institute on Early Childhood Development and Education. (2001). *New teacher for a new century: The future of early childhood professional preparation.* Jessup, MD: U.S. Department of Education.

Regional Educational Laboratories' Early Childhood Collaboration Network. (2002). *Continuity in early childhood: A framework for home, school, and community linkages.* Jessup, MD: U.S. Department of Education, Office of Education Research and Improvement.

CHAPTER 1

FAMILY INVOLVEMENT PROMOTES SUCCESS FOR YOUNG CHILDREN

A Review of Recent Research

Heather Weiss, Margaret Caspe, and M. Elena Lopez

The evidence is clear. Substantial research now supports and demonstrates that family involvement is critical for young children's socioemotional and cognitive growth. In addition, an increasing body of intervention evaluations demonstrates that family involvement processes can be strengthened with positive results for young children and their school readiness. Early childhood practitioners also recognize now more than ever that their services alone cannot prepare children for kindergarten; they need the support of families and communities. In order to gain this support, practitioners need to encourage the family involvement processes that research and evaluation have shown to be beneficial for children's learning and socioemotional development. Thus, the purpose of this chapter is twofold: (1) to review recent research on family involvement processes related to young children's academic and social growth while highlighting evidence-based

Promising Practices for Partnering with Families in the Early Years, pages 1–19
Copyright © 2008 by Information Age Publishing
All rights of reproduction in any form reserved.

family involvement program models that impact positively young children's development, and (2) to provide suggestions for early childhood practitioners for new approaches about how to work more effectively with families.

METHOD

In order to examine the family involvement processes related to young children's academic and social achievement, the authors reviewed outcome-based empirical research published, for the most part, from 1999 to 2005. Outcome-based investigations were defined as those that measured family involvement and then linked family involvement to outcomes considered representative of young children's positive growth and development. The electronic catalogues ERIC, Education Abstracts, PsychINFO, SocioFILE, and Current Contents were searched using a combination of keywords including "parent," "family," "home," "teacher," and "school." Searches were further refined to include specific terms such as "family–school relationships," "parent–teacher cooperation," and "family involvement." As stated previously, only those articles that focused on family involvement as it related to child outcomes were integrated into this review.

The articles included were published in peer-reviewed journals, mainly from the fields of developmental psychology and human development. The studies focused on various settings in which young children participated, including the home, preschool and Head Start programs, and the broader community. This review did not include other environments such as child care or family day care because few studies have investigated how family involvement in these settings relates to children's outcomes. The majority of the studies were conducted using experimental, quasi-experimental, longitudinal, or correlational designs. Some qualitative studies that described the family involvement practices associated with children's school achievement were included, as were seminal articles and books published prior to 1999. All journal articles and books were summarized and coded for methodology, family involvement practices, and children's outcomes. Although this review focuses on birth to age 5, the majority of studies concentrated on age 3–5 years, in which the outcomes measured were aligned with goals generally related to school readiness.

In addition, evaluation reports of the four programs featured in this review were examined. These programs were chosen because they had a clear and substantial evidence base; however, they do not represent the universe of rigorously evaluated family involvement initiatives. These reports came from various sources including journals, the Internet, and unpublished manuscripts from Harvard Family Research Project's evaluation database.

FAMILY INVOLVEMENT PROCESSES AND PROGRAMS THAT PROMOTE POSITIVE OUTCOMES IN EARLY CHILDHOOD

Early childhood—in this case, defined as the period from birth to age 5—is a time of life during which significant transformations take place. The newborn infant, equipped with basic reflexes, develops into an active, curious child capable of walking, talking, and pretending. Children's vocabulary increases rapidly, and they acquire the ability to remember experiences, sustain attention, count, and recognize letters. Through interactions with adults and peers, young children develop concepts of self and worth, improve emotional self-regulation, and form their first friendships (Brooks-Gunn, Fulgini, & Berlin, 2003). In short, the early years are important because they are the period during which children acquire the socioemotional and cognitive skills that serve as the foundation for later learning. Moreover, these years are the time when parents' beliefs about their children's abilities are shaped and when children's own academic self-concepts begin to form (Harter, 1999).

In order for children to reach these milestones, it is necessary to match a young child's developing needs, a parent's attitudes and practices, and an early childhood program's expectations and support of family involvement. Three family involvement processes emerged from the articles in this review for creating this match: *parenting, home–program relationships,* and *responsibility for learning outcomes.* (See Figure 1.1.) The term "process" signifies that family involvement is a dynamic series of actions and beliefs that change over time as a joint function of the characteristics of the developing child and the environments in which the family involvement processes take place (Bronfenbrenner, 1986). *Parenting* processes refer to the attitudes, values, and practices of parents in raising young children. *Home–program relationships* are the formal and informal connections between the family and educational setting. *Responsibility for learning* is the parenting process that places emphasis on activities in the home and community that promote learning skills in the young child.

While the three processes described provide a framework by which to organize the research, readers must keep in mind that family involvement includes other processes beyond those described in this chapter. For example, parent leadership, community organizing, and participation in early childhood program decision making are not represented in this review. This is not because these forms of family involvement lack value. Instead, their omission reflects the shortage of empirical research linking these activities to young children's outcomes. As already explained, this review focused deliberately on those family involvement processes that research has

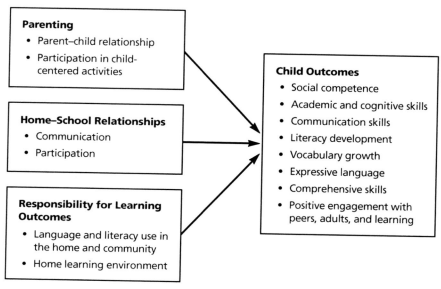

Figure 1.1   Processes of family involvement and young children's outcomes.

shown to empirically relate to or to cause young children's positive learning and development.

Parenting in Early Childhood

Parenting is the family involvement process that includes the attitudes, values, and practices of parents in raising young children. Nurturing, warm, and responsive parent–child relationships and parental participation in child-centered activities relate to positive learning outcomes in early childhood.

Parent–Child Relationships

Nurturing relationships provide an emotional refuge for children, fostering the development of a healthy sense of belonging, self-esteem, and well-being (National Institute of Child Health and Human Development Early Child Care Research Network, 2004). When parents are sensitive and responsive to children's needs and emotions, children are more likely to become socially competent and to show better communication skills (Connell & Prinz, 2002). Warm, reciprocal parent–child interactions and fewer life stresses in the home facilitate children's prosocial behavior and ability to concentrate (Lamb-Parker, Boak, Griffin, Ripple, & Peay, 1999).

Participation in Child-Centered Activities

Parent participation in child-centered activities is also an important component of parenting that makes a difference for children's development. Children who play at home and whose parents understand the importance of play in development are likely to demonstrate prosocial and independent behavior in the classroom (Fantuzzo & McWayne, 2002). For example, children's play abilities in the home are related to positive play interactions with their peers at school, motivation to learn, task persistence, and autonomy (Fantuzzo & McWayne, 2002). In addition, parent participation with their children in child-centered activities such as arts and crafts is associated with children's literacy development (Nord, Lennon, Liu, & Chandler, 1999).

TEXT BOX 1.1   Putting Parenting Research to Practice

The Incredible Years Program, developed by Carolyn Webster-Stratton, applies research-proven parenting and teaching practices to strengthen young children's social competence and problem-solving abilities and reduce aggression at home and school. Incredible Years is a comprehensive program; it incorporates parenting components with teacher- and child-focused intervention strategies. Comprehensive programs such as Incredible Years are likely to be the most effective strategy to promote positive child outcomes (Smith, 1995). Thus, the Incredible Years Program is presented in four distinct formats:

- Parenting group sessions that focus on basic parenting skills, parental communication and anger management, and promoting children's academic skills
- A teacher classroom management series
- Two-hour weekly small therapy sessions for children
- Classroom lesson plans that can be delivered one to three times a week for teachers

Incredible Years has been tested with 3- to 8-year-old children with conduct problems as well as with 2- to 6-year-old children who are at high risk by virtue of living in poverty. The child program promotes children's social competence and reduces conduct problems; the parent program helps parents strengthen parenting skills and become more involved in their children's school activities; and the teachers' program strengthens classroom management skills, reduces classroom aggression, and improves teachers' ability to focus on students' social, emotional, and academic competence (Webster-Stratton, Reid, & Hammond, 2004).

www.incredibleyears.com

However, parenting is embedded in social and cultural contexts that influence parenting styles. Poverty is related to access to fewer social parenting supports, which in turn is associated with maternal depression and less nurturing parenting behavior (Marshall, Noonan, McCartney, Marx, & Keefe, 2001; McLoyd, 1995). Moreover, parent–child activities are culturally influenced such that activities that are characteristic of one ethnic group might not be characteristic of another (Arzubiaga, Ceja, & Artiles, 2000; Barbarin, 2002; Delgado-Gaitan, 2001). For example, teaching letters, words, songs, and music is more characteristic of black non-Hispanic groups, whereas reading and telling stories is more typical of white non-Hispanic groups (Nord et al., 1999). In addition, given differences in social contexts, the same activities may have different effects. Interventions to support parenting include home visits (see Text Box 1.2), as well as group-centered activities in early childhood settings.

Home–Program Relationships

In the early childhood years, the home–program relationship refers to the formal and informal connections between families and their young children's educational settings. Both participation in preschool-based activities and regular communication between families and teachers are related to young children's outcomes. Parent participation practices can include attending parent–teacher conferences, participating in extended class visits, and helping with class activities. Such participation is associated with child language, self-help, social, motor, adaptive, and basic school skills (Marcon, 1999). Maintaining relationships with fathers is important too. In a study of low-income African American fathers, involvement in Head Start was associated with higher levels of children's emotion regulation (Downer & Mendez, 2005).

The frequency of parent–teacher contact and involvement at the early childhood education site is also associated with preschool performance (Izzo, Weissberg, Kasprow, & Fendrich, 1999). Parents who maintain direct and regular contact with the early educational setting and who experience fewer barriers to involvement have children who demonstrate positive engagement with peers, adults, and learning (McWayne, Hampton, Fantuzzo, Cohen, & Sekino, 2004). In addition, teachers' reports of positive parental attitudes and beliefs about preschool are associated with fewer behavior problems and higher language and math skills among children (Rimm-Kauffman, Pianta, Cox, & Bradley, 2003).

TEXT BOX 1.2 Home Visiting

Home visiting is a service delivery mode that reaches thousands of families and young children, especially under the age of 3, each year. Home visiting programs vary in magnitude and specific goals, but all share the central philosophy that parents and children benefit when early childhood practitioners engage with families and children in the home environment and provide services to parents and children together. Examples of six national programs include Early Head Start, Healthy Families America, Home Instruction for Parents of Preschool Youngsters (HIPPY), the Nurse Family Partnership, Parents As Teachers, and the Parent–Child Home Program. Although there is research demonstrating that participation in home visiting can affect children's outcomes including higher birth weight, early literacy skills, and social competence and provide benefits to parents, there is also evidence that disputes the magnitude and effect of the practice (see Daro, 2006, for a review). In a recent article, Raikes and colleagues (2006) identified three different components of parent involvement in home visiting services that practitioners can consider when providing these services:

- *Quantity of involvement.* This aspect of family involvement in home visiting pertains to the amount of participation and engagement parents have in the program including the number of home visits, duration of time in the program, intensity of home visits, and the average length of each visit.
- *Quality of engagement.* This aspect of family involvement in home visiting refers to the style and type of parents' engagement including their enthusiasm for the program.
- *Visit content.* This aspect of family involvement in home visiting includes the percent of time of the home visit spent on child-focused activities versus parent-centered activities.

The authors found that the length of time that families were involved in the program and the proportion of time during visits devoted to child-focused activities predicted positive outcomes for both children and families (Raikes et al., 2006). They suggest that programs and their evaluators can measure multiple aspects of home visits and sharpen and refine child-focused activities.

To learn more about home visiting and the Home Visit Forum, a field-building strategy for improving the conceptual clarity and quality of home visitation services, go to

www.gse.harvard.edu/hfrp/projects/homevisit/index.html

Outcomes Over Time

Not only do strong home–program relationships matter for children's outcomes during the early childhood years, but the benefits persist over time. For example, family involvement activities such as keeping in touch with a teacher, volunteering in the classroom, and attending school activities were related to children's promotion after kindergarten into the first grade (Mantizicopoulos, 2003). More frequent parental engagement in program activities is important—probably because it contributes to parents' greater knowledge of the early childhood program and familiarity with school experiences. Moreover, parental presence in early childhood programs may model for the child the importance of schooling.

The home–program relationship can buffer the negative impacts of poverty on the academic and behavioral outcomes of poor children. For example, children of low-income parents who participated in Chicago Child–Parent Centers (CPC) were more prepared for kindergarten, were less likely to be referred to special education, and later had higher rates of eighth-grade reading achievement and high school completion and lower rates of grade retention (Barnard, 2004; Clements, Reynolds, & Hickey, 2004; Graue, Clements, Reynolds, & Niles, 2004; Miedel & Reynolds, 1999).

Why do the benefits of home–program relationships sustain over time? One possible answer is that family involvement in early childhood sets the stage for involvement in future school settings. For instance, family involvement in the CPC program during children's early years was associated with greater parent involvement in children's elementary school years, which in turn was related with positive youth outcomes in high school (Ou, 2005). Thus, early positive patterns in the home–program relationship bridge children's experiences over time and across educational settings.

Transitions to Formal Schooling

Because of the importance of linkages across settings and over time, policymakers, practitioners, and researchers recently have begun to focus their attention on the period of transition from preschool to formal schooling. Although only a limited body of research in this area has focused on which transition practices relate to specific child outcomes, there is growing consensus that both early childhood settings and elementary schools have a responsibility to support families and help them to sustain their family involvement trajectories. For example, Schulting, Malone, and Dodge (2005) found that kindergarten transition policies in the fall of kindergarten had a modest but positive effect on students' academic achievement and on parent-initiated school involvement over the course of the year. These policies included, but were not limited to, sending or phoning home information about the kindergarten program, inviting parents and children to visit kindergarten prior to the start of the school year, having teachers visit students' homes, and offering orientation sessions. Furthermore, the effect of transition practices on academic achievement was stronger for children from average- or low-income families than for children from more affluent backgrounds (Schulting et al., 2005).

Unfortunately, as children transition to kindergarten, teacher and family contact decreases, and there is a shift away from parent-initiated communication (Fantuzzo, Tighe, & Childs, 2000; Rimm-Kauffman & Pianta, 2000). Logistical barriers (e.g., schools generating kindergarten class lists late in the summer, no summer salary for teachers, little teacher training in this area, etc.) hinder ideal transition practices (Early et al., 2001). Yet schools that provide more opportunities for family involvement and occasions for nontraditional contact—such as home visits, parent discussion groups, parent resource rooms, and home lending libraries—enjoy increased levels of family participation (Ramey et al., 2000).

Responsibility for Learning Outcomes

Responsibility for learning outcomes refers to an aspect of parenting that involves placing emphasis on educational activities that promote school success. In early childhood, this family involvement process tends to focus on how parents can support children's language and literacy and create a home learning environment.

Language and Literacy Use in the Home and in the Community

Reading to children is often recognized as the most important activity parents can do with their children at home. Children whose parents read to them recognize letters of the alphabet and write their names sooner (Nord et al., 1999). Direct parent-teaching activities—such as showing children how to write words in developmentally appropriate ways—are linked to children's ability to identify letters and connect letters to speech sounds (Haney & Hill, 2004). However, reading is not the only pathway to a strong language environment. Mothers who use more complex sentences and a wider range of different words in their everyday conversations and stories have children with richer expressive language and higher scores on literacy-related tasks in kindergarten (Britto & Brooks-Gunn, 2001; Tabors, Roach, & Snow, 2001).

**TEXT BOX 1.3   Supporting Home–School Relationships
Over Time**

Chicago Child–Parent Centers (CPC) have been administered by the
Chicago public schools since 1967 and are funded through the Elementary and Secondary Education Act of 1965. One of the programs cited
most frequently by policymakers and researchers building the argu-
ment for universal pre-K, the CPC program provides preschool education for low-income children from age 3 through third grade, as well as
a variety of family support services inside and outside the centers.

Although home visitation is provided, most family support activities
are directed toward enhancing involvement in children's education at
home and in school. Involvement may include a wide variety of activities, such as parents volunteering as classroom aides, interacting with
other parents in the center's parent resource room, participating in
educational workshops and courses, attending school events, accom-
panying classes on field trips, and attending parent–teacher meetings.
This involvement strengthens parenting skills, vocational skills, and
social supports.

Studies have indicated that CPC is effective in promoting both family and child development outcomes. Relative to a matched control
group of children, CPC preschool participation was associated with
greater parent involvement in and satisfaction with children's schooling and higher expectations for children's educational attainment
(Reynolds, 2000). Both preschool participation and preschool plus
school-age participation were associated with greater school achievement and lower rates of school remediation services. Moreover,
preschool participation was consistently associated with higher rates
of high school completion and lower rates of official juvenile arrest
for violent and nonviolent offenses (Reynolds, Temple, Robertson, &
Mann, 2001).

www.aecf.org/publications/advocasey/spring2002/chicago.htm

Families, however, differ in the extent to which they expose their children to language. In their seminal research, Hart and Risley (1995) found
that children from families with higher socioeconomic status show significantly greater rates of vocabulary growth and demonstrate richer forms of
language use and interaction than children from families living in poverty.
They conclude that the achievement gap begins even before preschool, in
the home environments of children from birth to age 3, and they recom-
mend that families living in poverty receive the parenting supports that can
promote the literacy development of their children. In fact, responsibility
for learning activities, such as reading to children and participating in com-

munity activities including making library visits, going on trips to the zoo, having picnics, and attending and taking part in sporting events, has the power to alter the influence of poverty on children's language and literacy development (Foster, Lambert, Abbott-Shim, McCarty, & Franze, 2005).

Home Learning Environment

Beyond language and literacy, the type of learning environment families establish for their young children also contributes to their growth and development. For example, children whose parents place a heavier emphasis on academic stimulation, the role of curiosity in learning, and provide more interest-related materials in the home are more likely to develop long-term individual interests than children of parents who do not provide these environments (Leibham, Alexander, Johnson, Neitzel, & Reis-Henrie, 2005).

TEXT BOX 1.4   Promoting Reading in the Home through Family Literacy Programs

Family literacy programs today are widely recognized as one way to help parents take an active role in their children's literacy development. One new initiative, the Early Authors Program, promotes early bilingual literacy in preschool children by providing early childhood educators with an example of how children's literacy, identity, and self-esteem can be supported while respecting their families' funds of knowledge and home languages. Inspired by the work of Alma Flor Ada and Isabel Campoy with school-age children, the Early Authors Program was developed, piloted, and evaluated in Miami–Dade County, Florida, by Judith Bernhard.

Family and center-based child care settings are provided with a digital camera, color printer, computer, and laminating equipment, and together children, parents, and educators author books in both English and the home languages of the children. The books are based on family histories, the children's lives, and the children's interests, and family photographs and children's drawings are used to illustrate the books. Through the program, parents have opportunities to talk with teachers and bring home new ideas, resources, and techniques for incorporating literacy into their everyday home activities. The program has been evaluated with 800 families using a pretest/posttest randomized experimental design. The intervention was effective in increasing literacy practices in child care centers and increasing language and literacy scores of 3- and 4-year-olds (Bernhard & Cummins, 2004).

www.ryerson.ca/~bernhard/early.html

**TEXT BOX 1.5 Promoting Responsibility for Learning
in the Home and in the Community**

Raising a Reader is a nonprofit and supporting organization of
Peninsula Community Foundation, a community association located
in San Mateo, California. The Raising a Reader mission is to foster
healthy brain development, parent–child bonding, and early literacy
skills critical for school success by engaging parents in a routine of daily
"book cuddling" with their children from birth through age 5. Raising
a Reader is based on the premise that when parents establish a reading routine with their children, family bonding time increases, as do
children's vocabulary and preliteracy skills.

Raising a Reader fosters a reading routine whereby children carry
bright red bags filled with high-quality picture books into their homes
each week. The books feature artwork, age-appropriate language,
and multicultural themes. During Literacy Nights, parents are taught
read-aloud strategies anchored to language development research and
storytelling.

Raising a Reader has spread to libraries, child care centers, Head
Start programs, teen mother programs, and home visiting nurse programs in 72 communities, 24 states, Mexico, Botswana, and Malaysia. A
variety of independent evaluations show that Raising a Reader significantly improves family reading behavior and kindergarten readiness,
especially for low-income, non-English-speaking families. Raising a
Reader has been shown to increase the amount of time parents spend
reading with their children, the number of visits parents and children
make to the library, and an increase in kindergarten readiness skills of
book knowledge, story comprehension, and print knowledge.

www.pcf.org/raising_reader/research.html

Fantuzzo, McWayne, and Perry (2004) demonstrated that when parents establish organized learning environments for their children including limit-
ing TV and video watching, keeping regular schedules for their children,
and establishing clear rules, children are more likely to develop the skills
necessary for school success.

Interestingly, responsibility for learning might be the family involvement
process that is most important for young children's outcomes. Fantuzzo
and his colleagues (2004) showed that practices associated with responsibility for learning (e.g., providing a place for educational activities, asking
a child about school, reading to a child) relate to children's motivation to
learn, attention, task persistence, and receptive vocabulary and to fewer
conduct problems, above and beyond the power of the home–program relationship.

IMPLICATIONS FOR EARLY CHILDHOOD PRACTITIONERS

This chapter demonstrates some of the ways by which family involvement is critical for children's success in the early years. Accordingly, several implications become apparent for practitioners as they strive to advance family involvement processes. These implications are based on the three family involvement processes that emerged from this review and have been shown to be effective by empirical research.

1. *Approach family involvement in multiple ways.* The three family involvement processes described in this chapter are important for children's success. Therefore, early childhood practitioners can and should approach family involvement in overlapping and multiple ways. For example, early childhood practitioners can help promote warm and nurturing parenting through workshops, trainings, and parent–child groups. (See Textbox 1.1). To develop home–program relationships, teachers can reach out to parents and invite their participation rather than wait for parents to approach them. They can also communicate frequently with parents about their young children's learning patterns and welcome opportunities for parents to visit the classroom. Moreover, early childhood practitioners can help parents take responsibility for their children's learning outcomes by sending home materials and ideas for activities that parents can do at home and in the community with their children. In addition, practitioners can attempt to incorporate responsibility for learning processes into their own classroom curriculum. For example, in the Early Authors Program (see Textbox 1.4), families were invited to read and share stories in the classroom in the style they used at home. This created an opportunity for two-way knowledge exchange between teachers and parents.

2. *Consider family involvement a continuum.* Early childhood educators and kindergarten teachers must recognize that families often enter their classrooms with histories of parenting experience and memories of prior relationships with child care providers and other early childhood educators. Teachers must actively invite parents to share both their child's and their own experiences in a previous setting, as well as how they would like to be involved in the present. In particular, kindergarten teachers can actively reach out to and become part of the early childhood programs in the community, while early childhood programs can form relationships with the elementary schools where children will be enrolled.

3. *Create mechanisms for smooth transitions.* Families are often the most consistent context in children's lives and provide a natural link between

the early childhood and elementary school learning environments. Early childhood practitioners must provide and sustain the kind of support and modeling needed to reduce stress for parents across transitions and give them clear strategies for positive interactions and relationships with their children upon entry into and exit from early childhood programs. Pamphlets and flyers can offer useful information but they are not sufficient. Parents need real opportunities to interact with early childhood providers and kindergarten teachers either in orientations or in classroom or home visits. School administrators can also alleviate logistical obstacles to transition practices by generating class lists early, providing professional development to kindergarten teachers regarding the importance of transition, and creating opportunities for parents and early childhood professionals to visit kindergarten classrooms in the spring and summer.

4. *Respect diversity.* This review also points to the importance of respecting and valuing the diversity of families and their family practices. For example, in this review teaching letters, words, songs, and music was more characteristic of black non-Hispanic groups, while reading and telling stories is more typical of white non-Hispanic groups (Nord et al., 1999). Teachers must uphold differences in home culture and practices while at the same time helping parents to understand the features of family involvement that are related to positive outcomes for children. For example, programs such as Early Authors build on parents' strengths and benefit children by giving parents a prominent role as their children's literacy teachers. (See Text Box 1.4.) Culturally responsive practice puts parents' skills, knowledge, and beliefs at the forefront, responds to families' interests and needs, and acknowledges differences among families as strengths that can be used to enrich children's growth and development, rather than deficits to be overcome.

5. *Partner with the community.* Early childhood and elementary school settings can work together to promote opportunities for family involvement within the community and across children's learning contexts. For example, classes and programs can take place in libraries, museums, zoos, and other community facilities. By connecting to resources in their communities early in their child's development, families can develop a broad network that can serve as a resource later in their child's life. For example, the Raising a Reader Program, which is often conducted in libraries, increases both the amount of time parents spend reading with their children and the number of visits parents and children make to the library. (See Text Box 1.5.)

6. *Keep current with family involvement research.* Because research is always evolving, early childhood educators must be informed of family in-

volvement studies, particularly as they pertain to new approaches to working with families. Early childhood educators can stay up-to-date by attending conferences, reading books such as this one, joining networks of like-minded professionals, and engaging in communities of practice. In addition, following appropriate coursework and practice, early childhood educators can begin to design and implement action research projects in their own classrooms to examine relationships with families.

CONCLUSION

Over the early childhood years, infants develop into young children able to communicate competently, play with others, sustain attention, regulate their emotions, and to enter formal schooling. The three family involvement processes of parenting, home–program relationships and responsibility for learning are critical to these developmental milestones. Early childhood practitioners have responsibilities to encourage these family involvement processes, and when they do, children, families, and early childhood programs can benefit from their outcomes.

For example, parenting that nurtures the parent–child relationship and emphasizes child-centered activities promotes young children's social competencies and communicative skills. Home–program relationships characterized by bilateral communication and opportunities for participation in early childhood program events are predictive of children's early literacy development and positive engagement with other children and adults, both during the early childhood years and into and throughout formal schooling. Last, when parents take responsibility for children's learning outcomes—including creating rich language and literacy settings and organized home-learning environments—children's language and literacy and prosocial behavior improve.

This review underscores the importance of considering these three family involvement processes as early childhood practitioners endeavor to create systematic, developmental, and comprehensive programs for all young children. With family involvement processes in place during the early childhood years, children will be poised for smooth transitions to kindergarten and for success throughout their schooling.

ACKNOWLEDGMENTS

This chapter was adapted from the Family Involvement Makes a Difference series by the Harvard Family Research Project and reprinted with their permission. Original research for this brief was made possible through the support of the W. K. Kellogg Foundation. We would also like to thank Celina Chatman of the University of Chicago, Lei-Anne Ellis and Lauren Leikin of the Agenda for Children, Lisa Klein of Hestia Advising, Christine McWayne of New York University, and Holly Kreider, Ellen Mayer, Priscilla M. D. Little, and Abby Weiss of Harvard Family Research Project for their insightful review and feedback.

REFERENCES

Arzubiaga, A., Ceja. M., & Artiles, A. J. (2000). Transcending deficit thinking about Latinos' parenting styles: Toward an ecocultural view of family life. In C. Tejeda, C. Martinez, Z. Leonardo, & P. McLaren (Eds.), *Charting new terrains of Chicana(o)/Latina(o) education* (pp. 93–106). Cresskill, NY: Hampton Press.

Barbarin, O. (2002). Ready or not!: African American males in kindergarten. In B. Bowman (Ed.), *Love to read: Preparing African American children for reading success* (pp. 1–15). Washington, DC: National Black Child Development Institute.

Barnard, W. M. (2004). Parent involvement in elementary school and educational attainment. *Children & Youth Services Review, 26*(1), 39–62.

Brooks-Gunn, J., Fuligni, A. S., & Berlin, L. J. (Eds.). (2003). *Early child development in the 21st century: Profiles of current research initiatives.* New York: Teachers College Press.

Bernhard, J. K., & Cummins, J. (2004, November). *Cognitive engagement and identity investment in literacy development among English language learners: Evidence from the Early Authors Program.* Paper presented at the English Language Learners Conference, National Center for Culturally Responsive Educational Systems, Scottsdale, AZ.

Britto, P. R., & Brooks-Gunn, J. (2001). Beyond shared book reading: Dimensions of home literacy and low-income African American preschoolers' skills. In J. Brooks-Gunn & P. R. Britto (Eds.), *New directions for child and adolescent development: Vol. 92. The role of family literacy environments in promoting young children's emerging literacy skills* (pp. 73–93). New York: Jossey-Bass.

Bronfrenbrenner, U. (1986). Ecology of the family as a context for human development: Research perspectives. *Developmental Psychology, 22*(6), 903–742.

Clements, M. A., Reynolds, A., J., & Hickey, E. (2004). Site-level predictors of children's school and social competence in the Chicago Child–Parent Centers. *Early Childhood Research Quarterly, 19,* 273–296.

Connell, C. M., & Prinz, R. J. (2002). The impact of childcare and parent–child interactions on school readiness and social skills development for low-income African American children. *Journal of School Psychology, 40*(2), 177–193.

Daro, D. (2006). *Home visitation: Assessing progress, managing expectations.* Chicago: Ounce of Prevention Fund and Chapin Hall Center for Children.

Delgado-Gaitan, C. (2001). *The power of community: Mobilizing for family and schooling.* New York: Rowman & Littlefield.

Downer, J. T., & Mendez, J. L. (2005). African American father involvement and preschool children's school readiness. *Early Education and Development, 16*(3), 317–340.

Early, D. M., Pianta, R. C., Taylor, L. C., & Cox, M. J. (2001). Transition practices: Findings from a national survey of kindergarten teachers. *Early Childhood Education Journal, 28,* 199–206.

Fantuzzo, J., & McWayne, C. (2002). The relationship between peer-play interactions in the family context and dimensions of school readiness for low-income preschool children. *Journal of Educational Psychology, 94*(1), 79–87.

Fantuzzo, J., McWayne, C., & Perry, M. (2004). Multiple dimensions of family involvement and their relations to behavioral and learning competencies for urban, low-income children. *School Psychology Review, 33*(4), 467–480.

Fantuzzo, J., Tighe, E., & Childs, S. (2000). Family Involvement Questionnaire: A multivariate assessment of family participation in early childhood education. *Journal of Educational Psychology, 92*(2), 367–370.

Foster, M. A., Lambert, R., Abbott-Shim, M., McCarty, F., & Franze, S. (2005). A model of home learning environment and social risk factors in relation to children's emergent literacy and social outcomes. *Early Childhood Research Quarterly, 20*(1), 13–36.

Graue, E., Clements, M. A., Reynolds, R. J., & Niles, M. D. (2004). More than teacher directed or child initiated: Preschool curriculum type, parent involvement and children's outcomes in the child parent centers. *Education Policy Analysis Archives, 12,* 1–38. Available at http://epaa.asu.edu/epaa/v12n72v12n72.pdf

Haney, M. H., & Hill, J. (2004). Relationships between parent-teaching activities and emergent literacy in preschool children. *Early Child Development and Care, 17*(3), 215–228.

Hart, B., & Risley, T. R. (1995). *Meaningful differences in the everyday experience of young American children.* Baltimore: Paul H. Brookes.

Harter, S. (1999). *The construction of self: A developmental perspective.* New York: Guilford Press.

Izzo, C. V., Weissberg, R. P., Kasprow, W. J., & Fendrich, M. (1999). A longitudinal assessment of teacher perceptions of parent involvement in children's education and school performance. *American Journal of Community Psychology, 27*(6), 817–839.

Lamb-Parker, F., Boak, A. Y., Griffin, K. W., Ripple, C., & Peay, L. (1999). Parent–child relationship, home learning environment, and school readiness. *School Psychology Review, 28*(3), 413–425.

Leibham, M. E., Alexander, J. M., Johnson, K. E., Neitzel, C. L., & Reis-Henrie, F. P. (2005). Parenting behaviors associated with the maintenance of preschoolers' interests: A prospective longitudinal study. *Applied Developmental Psychology, 26*(4), 397–414.

Mantizicopoulos, P. (2003). Flunking kindergarten after Head Start: An inquiry into the contribution of contextual and individual variables. *Journal of Educational Psychology, 95*(2), 268–278.

Marcon, R. (1999). Positive relationships between parent school involvement and public school inner-city preschoolers' development and academic performance. *School Psychology Review, 28*(3), 395–412.

Marshall, N. L., Noonan, A. E., McCartney, K., Marx, F., & Keefe, N. (2001). It takes an urban village: Parenting networks of urban families. *Journal of Family Issues, 22*(2), 163–182.

McLoyd, V. C. (1995). Poverty, parenting, and policy: Meeting the support needs of poor parents. In H. E. Fitzgerald, B. M. Lester, & B. Zuckerman (Eds.), *Children of poverty: Research, health, and policy issues* (pp. 269–303). New York: Garland.

McWayne, C., Hampton, V., Fantuzzo, J., Cohen, H. L., & Sekino, Y. (2004). A multivariate examination of parent involvement and the social and academic competencies of urban kindergarten children. *Psychology in the Schools, 41*(3), 363–377.

Miedel, W. T., & Reynolds, A. J. (1999). Parent involvement in early intervention for disadvantaged children: Does it matter? *Journal of School Psychology, 37*(4), 379–402.

National Institute of Child Health and Human Development, Early Child Care Research Network. (2004). Multiple pathways to early academic achievement. *Harvard Educational Review, 74*(1), 1–29.

Nord, C. W., Lennon, J., Liu, B., & Chandler, K. (1999). *Home literacy activities and signs of children's emerging literacy, 1993 and 1999* (NCES Publication No. 2000-026). Washington, DC: National Center for Education Statistics, U.S. Department of Education, Office of Educational Research and Improvement. Available at http://nces.ed.gov/pubsearch/pubsinfo.asp?pubid=2000026

Ou, S. (2005). Pathways of long-term effects of an early intervention program on educational attainment: Findings from the Chicago longitudinal study. *Applied Developmental Psychology, 26*(5), 578–611.

Raikes, H., Green, B. L., Atwater, J., Kisker, E., Constantine, J., & Chazen-Cohen, R. (2006). Involvement in Early Head Start home visiting services: Demographic predictors and relations to child and parent outcomes. *Early Childhood Research Quarterly, 21*, 2–24.

Ramey, S. L., Ramey, C. T., Philips, M. M., Lanzi, R. G., Brezausek, M. S., Katholi, C. R., et al. (2000). *Head Start children's entry into public school: A report on the National Head Start/Public Early Childhood Transition Demonstration Study.* Birmingham: Civitan International Research Center, University of Alabama. Available at http://www.acf.hhs.gov/programs/hs/ch_trans/reports/transition_study/trans_study_title .html

Reynolds A. J. (2000). *Success in early intervention: The Chicago Child–Parent Centers.* Lincoln: University of Nebraska Press.

Reynolds, A. J., Temple, J. A., Robertson, D. L., & Mann, E. A. (2001). Long-term effects of an early childhood intervention on educational achievement and juvenile arrest—a 15-year follow-up of low-income children in public schools. *Journal of American Medical Association, 285*, 2339–2346.

Rimm-Kauffman, S. E., & Pianta, R. C. (2000). An ecological perspective on the transition to kindergarten: A theoretical framework to guide empirical research. *Journal of Applied Developmental Psychology, 21*(5), 491–511.

Rimm-Kauffman, S. E., Pianta, R. C., Cox, M. J., & Bradley, R. H. (2003). Teacher-rated family involvement and children's social and academic outcomes in kindergarten. *Early Education and Development, 14*(2), 179–200.

Schulting, A. B., Malone, P. S., & Dodge, K. A. (2005). The effect of school-based kindergarten transition policies and practices on child academic outcomes. *Developmental Psychology, 41*(6), 860–871.

Smith, S. (1995). Two-generation programs. A new intervention strategy for directions for future research. In P. L. Chase-Landsdale & J. Brooks-Gunn (Eds), *Escape from poverty: What makes a difference for children?* (pp. 299–314). New York: Cambridge University Press.

Tabors, P. O., Roach, K. A., & Snow, C. E. (2001). Home language and literacy environment: Final results. In D. K. Dickinson & P. O. Tabors (Eds.), *Beginning literacy with language* (pp. 111–138). Cambridge, MA: Paul Brookes.

Webster-Stratton, C., Reid, M. J., & Hammond, M. (2004). Treating children with early-onset conduct problems: Intervention outcomes or parent, child, and teacher training. *Journal of Clinical Child and Adolescent Psychology, 33*(1), 105–124.

CHAPTER 2

LEARNING FROM THE FIELD OF EARLY INTERVENTION ABOUT PARTNERING WITH FAMILIES

Pamela J. Winton, Mary Jane Brotherson, and Jean Ann Summers

The importance of family–professional partnerships as an integral part of early childhood services has a long and venerable history in federal policies and initiatives, beginning with Head Start and continuing through the No Child Left Behind Act. The wide range of programs that emphasize family–professional partnerships includes Parents as Teachers, Even Start, Early Head Start and Head Start programs, early intervention for infants and toddlers with disabilities, early childhood special education services for children age 3–5, family-centered health services for children with special needs, and family-driven care for children's mental health (Brotherson, Summers, Bruns, & Sharp, 2008; Bruns & McCollum, 2002; File, 2001; Jeppson & Thomas, 1994; Johnson, 1995; Klass, 2003; Shelton & Stepanek, 1994; Trivette & Dunst, 2005).

Promising Practices for Partnering with Families in the Early Years, pages 21–40
Copyright © 2008 by Information Age Publishing
All rights of reproduction in any form reserved.

Different programs emphasize different aspects of family–professional partnerships. In Head Start, there has been a strong emphasis since its inception on family empowerment and families as decision-makers at program policy levels. In early childhood programs such as Parents as Teachers (PAT), the focus has been on parenting education and family support. In early intervention (EI) for infants and toddlers with disabilities, family-centered care has been an overarching approach for many years. This approach views the family as the focus for flexible and comprehensive services designed to build on family strengths and resources (McBride, Brotherson, Harvey, Whiddon, & Demmitt, 1993).

Regardless of differences in emphases, the importance of developing family–professional partnerships is alive and well in federal early childhood policies, both for children with special needs and for typically developing children. Many of the policies described are in part the result of legislative advocacy by various professional associations and parent networks with an interest in early childhood policy and services. Therefore, it is no surprise that the policies in many ways mirror recommended practices identified by professional associations (e.g., Division for Early Childhood of the Council for Exceptional Children and the National Association for the Education of Young Children).

A consideration in thinking about family partnerships is the national trend toward inclusion of young children with special needs in community-based early childhood care and education programs with the provision of specialized services being within natural environments (Dunst, Hamby, Trivette, Raab, & Bruder, 2000). This requires an integration of research and recommended practices related to family–professional partnership practices across both early childhood and early intervention/early childhood special education disciplines and programs.

A further consideration for early childhood professionals forming partnerships with families is how to be responsive to the demographic changes in the children under the age of 5 in this country. Nearly half are racial or ethnic minorities (U.S. Census Bureau, 2005). About 10% of public school students speak little or no English (National Center for Education Statistics, 2000). To be effective and supportive partners with families, it is critically important that early childhood practitioners understand and respect many cultural traditions, values, and beliefs, and engage in culturally responsive practices (Chen, McLean, Corso, & Bruns, 2004; Harry, 2002; Lynch, 2004).

The purpose of this chapter is to draw upon theory and research, primarily from early intervention/early childhood special education, to describe exemplary practices in building family–professional partnerships for *all* families. The first part of the chapter focuses on the theoretical framework underlying family involvement, which serves as the foundation for practices. Following that section, research and practical strategies for engaging in meaningful partnerships with families is described.

THEORETICAL FRAMEWORK

Knowledge of the ecology and culture of families as well as knowledge of family systems provide important theoretical perspectives for understanding the rationale and importance of family–professional partnerships.

Ecological Theory

Bronfenbrenner's developmental model for human behavior suggests that an individual develops within a context or ecology; the most immediate and earliest influence comes from the family (Bronfenbrenner, 1979). Individuals develop in relation to their family and home, school, community, and society, and each of these environments as well as interactions among these environments contribute to development. Bronfenbrenner's approach linked the family environment to human development and fueled an emphasis on the role of "parents as teachers" (Turnbull, Turnbull, Erwin, & Soodak, 2006). More recent research on early brain development (Shonkoff & Phillips, 2000) has helped to underscore the critical role of early experience—and thus the home environment—on children's development. Ecological theory thus supports the notion that enhanced parenting competence will maximize the quality of the home environment and have positive impacts on outcomes for children. A recent compilation of findings from a study funded by the National Institutes of Health demonstrates that family life has more influence on child development through preschool than does a child's experience in child care (National Institute of Child Health and Human Development, 2006), solidifying theory and common sense that families indeed matter.

Bronfenbrenner's work was extended by those who developed ecocultural theory (Bernheimer, Gallimore, & Weisner, 1990; Gallimore, Weisner, Bernheimer, & Guthrie, 1993) as a way of understanding the interaction of culture and environment in families. These theorists were particularly interested in assessing the impact of a child with special needs on the family and studied this by examining the degree to which family members must make changes in their lives to accommodate their child's needs. In the research that informed their theoretical model, they identified a number of tasks that families must accomplish on a daily basis. The tasks fall into the broad categories of parenting, instrumental and emotional support, marital role, material, domestic, health, and safety. According to this theory, it is the job of early childhood programs to help the family meet their child's needs within the context of the family's daily routines around these tasks, while maintaining as "normal" a life as possible. However, the nearly infinite combination of family, culture, community, and societal experiences means that every family makes these accommodations within its unique social and cultural context. Thus the recognition of parents as teachers of their children is supplemented by the understanding that families are the experts on their own family. Because only they can truly know and understand their own family's unique ecoculture, families have a critical role to serve as advocates, decision-makers, and trusted partners (Trivette & Dunst, 2005; Turnbull, Blue-Banning, Turbiville, & Park, 1999; Turnbull et al., 2006).

Family Systems Theory

Family systems theory provides a conceptual framework to help professionals assume a holistic view of the family. It is a core framework that describes the many ways that individuals in families are connected across time and space (Winton & Winton, 2005). Turnbull, Summers, and Brotherson (1984) originally applied family systems theory to a framework with four components: (1) *family characteristics* such as social, religious, and cultural identity; (2) *family interactions* among family members and extended family members (e.g., who interacts and how they interact); (3) *family functions* that include activities related to mobilizing resources and strengths to meet a variety of economic, physical, social, and spiritual needs (not unlike the tasks identified by Bernheimer et al., 1990, and Gallimore et al., 1993); and (4) *family life cycle*, which includes issues related to the stages of family life and transitions between each stage. Turnbull and colleagues (2006) have extended this work in *Families, Professionals, and Exceptionality: Positive Outcomes through Partnership and Trust,* which provides an understanding of family systems theory and its implications for family–professional partnerships within the field of special education. A contribution of family systems theory is that it demonstrates the interaction among all the parts of the system, which means that anything happening to one member of that system affects everyone in it. Thus family systems theory recognizes that a child's special needs create reciprocal needs for the entire family and, conversely, that achieving lasting change in child outcomes requires changes throughout the family to support progress for the child.

Theory provides an important underpinning to practice in several ways. It emphasizes that children's development depends on the capacity of their family to support their development and that families have a variety of tasks to accomplish (safety, health, marital, etc.) in addition to parenting their children. In other words, providing a broad range of support to families in ways that build their capacity to maintain a successful family system should be part of the mission for all early childhood programs. Theoretical knowledge of the ecology and family systems leads to establishing successful partnerships with families. The ultimate beneficiary of a successful partnership with the family is the child.

PRACTICES RELATED TO ESTABLISHING PARTNERSHIPS

Closing the gap between theory, research, and practice has been an elusive goal for the field of education for many years (Buysse & Wesley, 2006; Gersten & Woodward, 1992; Winton, 2006). Carl Dunst and his colleagues have been among the most productive researchers involved in examining the practices associated with effective family–professional partnerships and their relationship to family outcomes. Dunst (2002) has studied family-centered help-giving practices, which he defines as practices that do the following: treat families with dignity and respect; provide family members with information needed to make informed decisions and choices; promote active family involvement in procuring resources and supports; and involve practitioner responsiveness and flexibility to family requests and desires. The research by Dunst and colleagues has indicated that there are two distinct aspects of help-giving practices. They are relational practices, which they define as demonstrating respect, active listening, empathy for establishing relationships with families, and participatory practices, which they define as strategies for building competence, confidence, and capacity in families (Dunst, 2002). The following section describes research and practices related to each of these two dimensions as well as practices related to collaboration. Table 2.1 provides an overview of the partnership practices discussed.

Relational Practices Related to Establishing Partnerships

Much of the literature on family–professional partnerships emphasizes practices related to establishing relationships and trust (i.e., those that Dunst and his colleagues define as relational practices). Demonstrating an understanding of family perspectives (sometimes called "walking in their shoes") is the starting point for family–professional partnerships (Fialka, 2001; Muscott, 2002). In a qualitative study of families of children with disabilities and the practitioners who worked with them, Blue-Banning, Summers, Frankland, Nelson, and Beegle (2004) identified six broad themes of family–professional partnerships. The themes suggest that families and

TABLE 2.1   Overview of Partnership Practices

Partnership Practice	Definition	Characteristics
Relational practices related to establishing partnerships	Help-giving practices such as demonstrating respect, active listening, empathy for establishing relationships with families, and interpersonal and communication skills	• "walking in the families' shoes" • orientation to the whole family • friendliness with families • informal give-and-take exchanges of information • attending to issues of cultural diversity in families
Participatory practices related to establishing partnerships (building family capacity, confidence, and competence)	Help-giving practices such as responding to families' needs or requests for support, giving families choice and decision-making opportunities, and involving families in actively getting desired resources.	• focus on achievements and strengths, rather than deficits • use solution-oriented process • mobilize informal sources of support • ability to reflect on one's personal traditions and values • provide families with leadership and decision-making roles
Collaboration practices related to establishing partnerships	Collaborative practices such as relying on colleagues and allies in the community, building communities of practice, ensuring services and supports needed by families are available, and providing emotional supports to professionals	• help families navigate a maze of agency procedures • providing coordinated and intensive support to families facing multiple challenges • provide information about a wide range of possible resources in the community • help families connect with local or state parent resource centers

practitioners want partnerships characterized by respect and trust, effective communication, a mutual belief in parental and professional competencies, a sense of equality between parent and professional, and a sense of commitment to the well-being of the child and family. McWilliam, Tocci, and Harbin (1998) found that friendliness, responsiveness, orientation to the whole family, positiveness, and sensitivity were key components of establishing family–professional partnerships.

This collective research demonstrates the importance of interpersonal and communication skills as one of the cornerstones of developing positive partnerships. Showing a genuine interest in the child and the family at the beginning of forming a relationship is important in any early childhood context, whether it is a home visiting program, a clinic, or a classroom setting. Winton (1988) suggested four critical communication skills that affect a professional's ability to develop partnerships with families. These include:

1. *Listening*—Remembering that the greatest percentage of time when establishing partnerships with families should be spent in listening and learning about families and their children.
2. *Reflecting feelings*—Reflecting and acknowledging an understanding of the emotions and feelings expressed by the family is a way of conveying an understanding of the world as the family lives it.
3. *Reflecting content*—Summarizing and reflecting the content of the family member's message helps ensure a focus on the issues of importance to the family.
4. *Effective questioning*—Using questions in combination with other communication skills provides a deeper understanding of family interests and concerns.

Simply asking questions such as "Tell me about ____ (name of child)" or "What are her favorite things to do?" or "How does he let you know when he enjoys something?" are ways of opening a conversation and demonstrating interest. Beginning a parent–teacher conference or home visit by asking open-ended questions such as "How are things going?" or "How has your week been?" provides an opportunity for families to set the agenda by ensuring that the issues on families' minds are addressed immediately. These are not simply "icebreakers" designed to put parents at ease. Responding to the information that family members share—their concerns and interests—is equally important. Doing this may result in the professional having to abandon part of his or her own agenda; however, it is more likely that the family will feel they are an equal partner in the relationship when they have a chance to determine the focus of time spent with professionals. Being attuned to individual styles of communication is important. This includes amount of eye contact, physical posture, distance and contact, voice tone, and exchange of pleasantries and small talk. These differences may be cultural, ethnic, or geographic. Working with a cultural mediator (Moore & Pérez-Méndez, 2005), or individuals with intimate knowledge of specific groups with whom one is not familiar, is an excellent strategy for understanding the nonverbal aspects of communication that convey a listening and respectful stance. A cultural mediator is more than an interpreter, who translates spoken language, or a translator, who translates written documents. A cultural mediator is a link between the deep and sometimes hidden beliefs, values, and practices of the family and the program. As described by the Colorado Department of Education (2002), cultural mediators are valued members of the community with the following characteristics:

- an understanding of the language and culture of specific families;
- accepted by specific families with whom they work;
- skilled in interpersonal relations;
- proficient in oral and written English and proficient in the home language of the families with whom they work;
- able to maintain confidentiality; and
- open to learning their role and willing to take direction.

Understanding and using culturally sensitive communication practices contributes to a positive and welcoming climate that sets the stage for developing partnerships.

There are also structural aspects of forming partnerships with parents (e.g., arrangement of space and facilities, materials, logistics, organizational factors, etc.). The transition into a new program provides an important structural opportunity for establishing family partnerships. Providing home visits or setting up individual meetings with children and families for the purposes of getting acquainted are excellent ways to get to know a child and family and convey the message that families are important. Families in center-based programs have a strong interest in interacting with teachers through informal give-and-take exchanges of information at the beginning and end of the day (Winton & Turnbull, 1981). This provides an ongoing way for families to share concerns or successes as they occur on a daily basis. When children are transported to programs, daily interaction is more difficult, but still possible through notebooks or other communication strategies whereby teachers and parents share daily observations, comments, or questions.

Another structural aspect of developing a partnership is attending to issues related to the diversity of families served. Making materials available in the languages spoken by families and having access to translators indicates that programs and staff are truly welcoming of all families. As already mentioned, working with cultural mediators (Colorado Department of Education, Special Education Services Unit, 2002; Moore & Pérez-Méndez, 2005; Moore, Pérez-Méndez, & Boerger, 2006) is a specific way of supporting partnerships with all families. In a classroom setting ensuring that the artifacts, pictures, and activities reflect the linguistic, racial, cultural, and ability diversity of the children being served demonstrates very concretely that all families are welcome. For example, having pictures of fathers as well as mothers on the walls of a center conveys the message that fathers are welcome.

Having the means to help families connect with other families who share common interests and concerns through informal means or through local Parent-to-Parent programs in cases when parents have a child who has been diagnosed with a disability (Santelli, Poyadue, & Young, 2001) is another strategy for responding to parents' immediate needs for information and support. This should be done with sensitivity and in response to parents' interest in pursuing this kind of contact. Creating spaces in center-based programs where families feel welcome to look at resources or have coffee and talk together engenders a sense of belonging, involvement, and partnership. This provides a way for families to go about these connections in ways that fit their timetable and interest level.

These are examples of practices that convey the message to families that they are respected and that a partnership relationship is what is desired and valued by the program and the staff. However, the real work comes in building and deepening that partnership over time.

Participatory Practices for Building Family–Professional Partnerships

Participatory practices involve responding to families' needs or requests for support by building the confidence, competence, and capacity of parents. This approach may be difficult for practitioners who were trained in an expert model in which they are expected to be the sole source for answers and expertise. If one recognizes that families are the constant in children's lives and are the adults who will be there for their children for the "long haul," it makes sense (and reflects the theoretical frameworks described earlier) to engage in practices that build family members' confidence and competence in parenting. Dunst et al. (2000) described this form of help-giving as giving families choice and decision-making opportunities, and involving families in actively procuring or obtaining desired resources, supports, and goals. The ability to engage in *participatory* practices for building family capacity builds on the relational skills described earlier. However, this requires an additional set of help-giving skills related to being non-judgmental and using communication skills that go beyond listening and reflecting. People generally have an extremely positive response to practitioners who are nonjudgmentally interested in them and their situations and who focus on strengths, achievements, and desires rather than deficits. Winton (Winton, 1996; Winton & Winton, 2005) has described solution-oriented questions as a strategy to use when talking with families about areas of concern. Rather than asking about problems, it is helpful to focus on the times when events of interest have gone well. For instance, after reflecting and fully understanding a statement from a parent who registers a concern, the practitioner might consider exploring with the parent any solutions the family has tried by asking: "What have you found that worked or helped in that situation?" This provides valuable information about approaches they have tried that either worked or did not work. Knowing what did not work helps avoid making suggestions that lead to: "We already tried that." Questions such as: "Have there been times when things have gone well in regard to whatever situation?" are effective in opening up the possibilities of exploring successes (even if they are few and far between). This can lead toward an exploration of strategies or solutions that fall within the existing capacity of families through questions such as "What is happening when things are going well?" This kind of dialogue allows practitioners to support the adaptive potential of families.

It is important to remember that some aspects of professional practice, such as home visiting, intervene in some of the most personal of family practices such as feeding, toileting, sleeping, and discipline (Barrera, 2004; Gonzalez-Mena, 2005; Lynch & Hanson, 2004; Oser & Ayankoya, 2000; Parette & Brotherson, 2004). Developing partnerships is relatively easy when families and professionals share the same basic values and beliefs about childrearing and parenting. However, when differences in opinion arise, which frequently happens when values and beliefs collide, it takes extraordinary skill for professionals to refrain from being critical and judgmental of parents. Too many times, professionals think that they have the answers and the "correct way" of parenting in these areas. Thorp and Sánchez (2008) make the important point that the tangible representations of culture (e.g., dress, holidays, artifacts) are easier to ascertain than the intangible differences associated with culture. These intangible aspects of culture (meaning deeply held but not always visible values and beliefs) can lead to difficulties in partnership relationships. Using solution-oriented questions, such as asking parents to describe the ways that they address challenges, or asking family members to describe times when something that is a challenge is going well, are communication strategies for tapping into family beliefs about parenting and family expertise. It is tempting for professionals to jump in with answers prior to exploring the strengths and strategies that family members have at their disposal or that work within their belief system. Beliefs are very difficult to change, which is the reason why understanding and working within belief systems is a critical aspect of building partnerships. Perhaps "things go well" when an extended family member, such as a grandparent, comes to help; others may seek solutions to challenges by consulting with a spiritual adviser. That information provides the professional with valuable information about the families' extended network of support, making it possible for the professional to draw upon and include these resources in educational planning and support. This information is also helpful in understanding sources of advice, which may at times conflict with professional opinions. Using "skilled dialogues" for exploring perspectives, sharing expertise, and reaching understanding and acceptance of differences is a communication strategy described by Barrera and Corso (2003) for finding what they define as the "third space" that allows for partners to move forward together in spite of differences in how they view things. When values and beliefs conflict, it is sometimes helpful to think about shared interests as a way of finding common ground. A genuine interest in a child's growth, development, and happiness is one shared by professionals and families and provides a starting point and ending point for difficult discussions where a variety of perspectives about solutions to challenges may exist. As long as a family's solution does not jeopardize seriously a child's well-being, it is important to show interest, curiosity, and willingness to explore the solution with them. This keeps dialogue open and provides a chance to develop a positive relationship with the family. Over time, once trust is built, solutions may emerge as a result of the partnership that would not have been available to the family or professional working on their own.

Another advantage to using solution-oriented questions, mentioned earlier, is that professionals can learn about informal sources of support that could be enhanced or enlisted into the process of mobilizing resources. Informal support available from family, friends, neighbors, or religious communities has been shown by research to be highly valued by parents (Crnic, Greenberg, Ragozin, Robinson, & Basham, 1983). The advantages afforded by informal supports are innumerable. Usually, trust has already been established. Also, there are chances for reciprocity, meaning that families may be able to give support in turn and therefore may be in a position to give help as well as receive it, which is empowering. It is also important to recognize that some families at some points in time may be searching for professional expertise and want nothing more than to hear an expert's advice. Some families may come from a background where respect for authority is tantamount. Some families may have a limited understanding of English. In these cases family members may automatically agree with professionals or fail to ask questions even when they disagree with decisions or when they do not understand what is happening (Gonzalez-Mena, 2001; Park & Turnbull, 2001). These are reasons why cultural mediators, described earlier, are important allies in building and sustaining family partnerships. Also, the ability to establish trusting partnerships with families of diverse cultural backgrounds requires increased self-awareness, including the ability to reflect on one's personal traditions and values (Harry, 2002; Harry, Kalyanpur, & Day, 1999; Muscott, 2002). This is why diversity training usually begins with an exploration of participants' own culture, leading to a recognition that assumptions about seemingly "universal" values may in fact be part of the practitioner's culture and may not be shared by the families he or she is serving. Ongoing supervision, mentoring, or other forms of professional development and support are important aspects of building the capacity of professionals and programs for forming effective partnerships with families.

The structural aspects of building family capacity, confidence, and competence include providing families with opportunities to serve in leadership and decision-making roles. Head Start has a long history of involving parents in program governance through parent policy councils (Lamb-Parker et al., 1997; Schumacher, 2003). The Federal Interagency Coordinating Council, whose role was to develop guidelines for early intervention policy across multiple federal agencies, issued a set of principles related to the practice of involving family members at all levels of policy and service delivery planning, as a sign of their commitment to families as leaders (Federal Interagency Coordinating Council, 2000). The National Professional Development Center on Inclusion (2007) published a set of recommendations related to meaningfully including family members in state-level policy and planning groups. Winton (2000) suggested that early childhood programs consider having "accountability councils" consisting of staff and parents who engage in program self-study for the purpose of building quality in ways that are unique to the community and families being served. Since families and children are the ultimate beneficiaries of educational programs and services, their role as partners in evaluation and policy decisions seems logical. It is important to remember that not every family member wants this role. Parents who do assume leadership roles often need orientation, preparation, and support to engage actively and meaningfully in the activities. However, having these options for involvement are an important part of building program quality and forming partnerships with families.

Practices Related to Collaboration across Multiple Agencies and Disciplines

A third area where skills and knowledge related to family partnerships are essential is in the area of collaboration. Practitioners often work in isolation and feel they have little support for challenges they face on a daily and ongoing basis. Being able to rely on colleagues and allies in the community is an important way of reducing this sense of isolation and building skills related to family partnerships.

Building and sustaining collaborative partnerships with other practitioners is also important in terms of working with families, especially when families have needs that benefit from coordinated efforts across programs.

While all families face challenges in life, some families face multiple crises that consume their energy and sense of competence (McBride & Brotherson, 1997). These families require more intensive investments of emotional, informational, and especially material support. The potential for practitioners to encounter a family with multiple challenges has increased over the last decade. For example, the number of children in extreme poverty (i.e., below an annual income of $7,610) has increased by 20 percent since 2000, and more than one out of every six children in the United States lives below the poverty line (Children's Defense Fund, 2006). The challenges associated with poverty include depression, substance abuse, violence, malnourishment, and increased risk of injury or environmental toxins (Hanson & Carta, 1996). All of these risk factors mean an increased risk that children in poverty will acquire a disability (Fujiura & Yamaki, 2000; Park, Turnbull, & Turnbull, 2002). Multiple challenges may result in repetitive cycles of family crisis, a sense of learned helplessness, and alienation from help-giving professionals (Summers, Templeton-McMann, & Fuger, 1997).

Families with many challenges require more intensive family support and more time and effort to engage them in a meaningful partnership. They may need lengthy and time-consuming efforts to build trust and rapport before work with a child may even begin (Summers et al., 1997). Working with multiple agencies and disciplines, which is often the experience for families at risk or for those with children with disabilities, can be stressful (Lessenberry & Rehfeldt, 2004); helping families by supporting collaboration across programs can reduce some of the confusion they may experience. In addition, families may be unaware of possible resources for themselves or their child (Blue-Banning et al., 2004); therefore, collaboration can provide practitioners with information about a wide range of possible resources in the community they can pass along to families. Helping families collaborate with their multiple providers and navigate a maze of agency procedures is important. Families may need more than a name and phone number to help them access needed services. A knowledgeable service coordinator who can win the family's trust and "walk them through" the procedures involved in accessing services is a critical member of the team of professionals who may be available to support families.

Programs with great potential for providing support and services for families are local or state parent resource centers (i.e., programs staffed by parents that offer an array of information, training, and support) (Technical Assistance Alliance for Parent Centers, 2006). Families who have children with disabilities may access in every state a Parent Training and Information Center, focused on providing information and support to parents to participate effectively in the special educational system. In some communities with large numbers of unserved or underserved families (members of minority groups and/or families with poverty backgrounds), programs called Community Parent Resource Centers (CPRCs) have a similar mission to help families from diverse backgrounds access and participate in early intervention and special education programs (Technical Assistance Alliance for Parent Centers, 2006).

For families of typically developing children, the U.S. Department of Education funds Parental Information and Resource Centers (PIRCs), which provide information to enhance parent involvement with education programs. This program is particularly focused on helping schools strengthen partnerships with families and to help families understand and participate in the choices offered by the No Child Left Behind Act. The law requires grantees to use at least 50 percent of funds to serve areas with high concentrations of families with low incomes and a minimum of 30 percent of funds must support early childhood parent education programs such as Parents as Teachers (Parental Information and Resource Centers, 2007). Finally, child care resource and referral centers can offer parents an array of information on resources in the community. It is important for early childhood programs to have close links with all these supports.

In cases when families have multiple challenges, providers must be patient and persistent, be able to set aside their own feelings, connect the family to a variety of resources, and be absolutely reliable in their dealings with the family, even when the parents are not reliable themselves (Brookes, Summers, Thornburg, Ispa, & Lane, 2006). It is important for supervisors and administrators to recognize and honor the frustrations that such a slow engagement process involves for a practitioner; therefore, they need to provide opportunities to debrief and discuss feelings that may arise from working with parents who are so mired in crises that they appear uncooperative or self-destructive (Lane, 2005).

A final consideration in terms of building collaboration across agencies to ensure that families have access to services is the importance of those services actually being present. A recent analysis of four sources of knowledge (empirical, conceptual, narrative, and statutory) by Turnbull and colleagues (2007) indicated that the field of early childhood special education has focused almost exclusively on *how* families and professionals should interact, with insufficient attention on *what* services and supports should be available for families. The emphasis on process (the *how* of establishing partnerships) in the literature reviewed in this chapter reflects this emphasis. Turnbull et al. contend that services and supports needed by families may be lacking as a result of this inattention, and they call for increased emphasis on this important aspect of family–professional partnerships.

One way to support collaboration between colleagues and to address issues related to developing and delivering services is to build a "community of practice" (Wesley & Buysse, 2001; Winton, 2000). Communities of practice are groups of people who share a concern, goal, or passion and engage in discussion and reflection of each other's experiences to improve practices and build knowledge (Wesley & Buysse, 2001). Communities of practice focused on building partnerships with families can help build service systems in a collaborative fashion that translate into needed supports and services for families. A community of practice can also provide a sounding board to participants who want to ensure that their interactions with families are culturally responsive. Interagency or community-wide communities of practice that include meaningful representation by families can ensure continuous improvement in practitioner skills, coordination of services, and community resources.

SUMMARY

The ultimate outcome—that children grow and develop into productive, healthy, and happy adults—flows from families having an enhanced quality of life—and that goal is enhanced when professionals are able to form meaningful partnerships with diverse families. This chapter discusses a variety of practices that early childhood providers need to implement in order to develop those meaningful partnerships. In summary, early childhood providers, especially those in leadership positions, must strive to:

- Develop a mission statement that articulates the values and principles related to family–professional partnerships.
- Include family–professional partnership outcomes in efforts to monitor the quality of early education programs.
- Implement the *relational practices* related to establishing partnerships—such as active listening, respecting cultural differences, and connecting parents to "parent-to-parent."
- Implement *participatory practices* for building partnerships—strategies to support the confidence, competence, and capacity of parents—such as a "solution-oriented" process for helping families address areas of concern.
- Build collaborative partnerships across agencies and disciplines, especially when families have multiple challenges, to help reduce family stress and provide options for a wide array of possible resources.
- Ensure that services and supports needed by families are available.

It is important to recognize the valuable role family members themselves can play in helping early childhood practitioners understand the nuances of developing meaningful partnerships with the families. Drawing on the wisdom of family leaders who are part of national, state, or local family networks, such as Parent-to-Parent programs, can help professionals hone their skills and knowledge about building partnerships. Early childhood providers do not have to know the "right answers" in order to build meaningful partnerships with families. But they do need to know that parents are their partners in this process and can be their teachers as well as recipients of services. Simply put—it *is* a partnership.

REFERENCES

Barrera, I. (2004). Honoring differences: Essential features of appropriate ECSE services for young children from diverse sociocultural environments. *Young Exceptional Children Monograph Series No. 5,* 27–38.

Barrera, I., & Corso, R. (2003). *Skilled dialogue: Strategies for responding to cultural diversity.* Baltimore: Brookes.

Bernheimer, L. P., Gallimore, R., & Weisner, T. S. (1990). Ecocultural theory as the context for IFSP planning. *Journal of Early Intervention, 14*(3), 219–233.

Blue-Banning, M., Summers, J. A., Frankland, H. C., Nelson, L. L., & Beegle, G. (2004). Dimensions of family and professional partnerships: Constructive guidelines for collaboration. *Exceptional Children, 70*(2), 167–184.

Bronfenbrenner, U. (1979). *The ecology of human development: Experiments by nature and design.* Cambridge, MA: Harvard University Press.

Brookes, S., Summers, J. A., Thornburg, K., Ispa, J., & Lane, V. (2006). A qualitative exploration of factors influencing successful engagement of parents in Early Head Start. *Early Childhood Research Quarterly, 21,* 25–45.

Brotherson, M. J., Summers, J. A., Bruns, D. A., & Sharp, L. M. (2008). Family-centered practices: Working in partnership with families. In P. Winton, J. McCollum, & C. Catlett (Eds.), *Preparing effective professionals: Evidence and applications in early childhood and early intervention* (pp. 53–80). Washington, DC: Zero to Three.

Bruns, D. A., & McCollum, J. A. (2002). Mothers and medical professionals in the NICU: Examining the areas of caregiving, information exchange, and relationships. *Neonatal Network, 21*(7), 15–23.

Buysse, V., & Wesley, P. (Eds.). (2006). *Evidence-based practice in the early childhood field.* Washington, DC: Zero to Three.

Chen, D., McLean, M., Corso, R. M., & Bruns, D. (2004). Working together in early intervention: Cultural considerations in helping relationships and service utilization. In R. M. Corso, R. M. Santos, & S. A. Fowler (Eds.), *CLAS COLLECTION #2: Building healthy relationships with families* (pp. 39–58). Longmont, CO: Sopris West.

Children's Defense Fund. (2006). *Child poverty.* Retrieved February 21, 2006, from http://www.childrensdefense.org/familyincome/childpoverty/default.aspx

Colorado Department of Education, Special Education Services Unit. (2002, March). *Cultural mediators, translators, and interpreters.* Fact Facts. Retrieved February 21, 2006, from http://www.ced.state.co.us

Crnic, K. A., Greenberg, M. T., Ragozin, A. S., Robinson, N. M., & Basham, R. (1983). Effects of stress and social support on mothers and premature and full-term infants. *Child Development, 54,* 209–217.

Dunst, C. J. (2002). Family-centered practices: Birth through high school. *Journal of Special Education, 36*(3), 139–147.

Dunst, C. J., Hamby, D., Trivette, C. M., Raab, M., & Bruder, M. B. (2000). Everyday family and community life and children's naturally occurring learning opportunities. *Journal of Early Intervention, 23,* 151–164.

Early Childhood Outcomes Center. (2005, April). *Family and child outcomes for early intervention and early childhood special education.* Chapel Hill, NC: Author. Retrieved November 6, 2006, from http://www.fpg.unc.edu/~eco/pdfs/eco_outcomes_4-13-05.pdf

Federal Interagency Coordinating Council. (2000). Principles of family involvement. Retrieved November 7, 2006, from http://www.ed.gov/policy/speced/guid/idea/letters/2001-1/dearcolleague1022001ficc.pdf

Fialka, J. (2001). The dance of partnership: Why do my feet hurt? *Young Exceptional Children, 4*(2), 21–27.

File, N. (2001). Family–professional partnerships: Practice that matches philosophy. *Young Children, 56*(4), 70–74.

Fujiura, G. T., & Yamaki, K. (2000). Trends in demography of childhood poverty and disability. *Exceptional Children, 66,* 187–199.

Gallimore, R., Weisner, T., Bernheimer, L., & Guthrie, D. (1993). Family responses to young children with developmental delays: Accommodation activity in ecological and cultural context. *American Journal of Mental Retardation, 98,* 185–206.

Gersten, R., & Woodward, J. (1992). The quest to translate research into classroom practice: Strategies for assisting classroom teachers' work with at-risk students and students with disabilities. In D. Carnine & E. Dameenui (Eds.), *Higher cognitive functioning for all students* (pp. 201–218). Austin, TX: Pro-Ed.

Gonzalez-Mena, J. (2001). *Multicultural issues in child care.* Mountain View, CA: Mayfield.

Gonzalez-Mena, J. (2005). *Diversity in early care and education.* New York: McGraw-Hill.

Hanson, M. J., & Carta, J. J. (1996). Addressing the challenges of families with multiple risks. *Exceptional Children, 62*(3), 201–212.

Harry, B. (2002). Trends and issues in serving culturally diverse families of children with disabilities. *Journal of Special Education, 36*(3), 131–138.

Harry, B., Kalyanpur, M., & Day, M. (1999). Building cultural reciprocity with families: *Case studies in special education.* Baltimore: Brookes.

Individuals with Disabilities Education Improvement Act of 2004, 20 U.S.C. 1400 *et seq.*

Jeppson, E. S., & Thomas, J. (1994). *Essential allies: Families as advisors.* Bethesda, MD: Institute for Family-Centered Care.

Johnson, B. H. (1995). Newborn intensive care units pioneer family-centered change in hospitals across the country. *Zero to Three, 15*(6), 11–17.

Klass, C. S. (2003). *The home visitor's guidebook: Promoting optimal parent and child development* (2nd ed.). Baltimore: Brookes.

Lamb-Parker, F., Piotrkowski, C., Kessler-Sklar, S., Baker, A., Peay, L., & Clark, B. (1997). *Executive summary of the final report: Parent involvement in Head Start.* New York: National Jewish Council of Jewish Women, Center for the Child.

Lane, V. J. (2005). *Emotional labor in early intervention.* Unpublished doctoral dissertation, University of Missouri, Columbia.

Lessenberry, B. M., & Rehfeldt, R. A. (2004). Evaluating stress levels of parents of children with disabilities. *Exceptional Children, 70*(2), 231–244.

Lynch, E. W. (2004). Developing cross-cultural competence. In E. W. Lynch & M. J. Hanson (Eds.), *Developing cross-cultural competence: A guide for working with children and their families* (pp. 41–77). Baltimore: Brookes.

Lynch, E. W., & Hanson, M. J. (2004). Steps in the right direction: Implications for service providers. In E. W. Lynch & M. J. Hanson (Eds.), *Developing cross-cultural competence: A guide for working with children and their families* (pp. 449–466). Baltimore: Brookes.

McBride, S., & Brotherson, M. J. (1997). Guiding practitioners toward valuing and implementing family-centered practices. In P. J. Winton, J. A. McCollum, & C. Catlett (Eds.), *Reforming personnel preparation in early intervention: Issues, models, and practical strategies* (pp. 253–276). Baltimore: Brookes.

McBride, S., Brotherson, M. J., Harvey, J., Whiddon, D., & Demmitt, A. (1993). Implementation of family-centered services: Perceptions of families and professionals. *Journal of Early Intervention, 7*(4), 414–430.

McWilliam, R. A., Tocci, L., & Harbin, G. L. (1998). Family-centered services: Service providers' discourse and behavior. *Topics in Early Childhood Special Education, 18,* 206–221.

Moore, S., & Pérez-Méndez, C. (2005). Module 6: Parent & family involvement. In *English language learners with exceptional needs.* Golden, CO: Meta Associates.

Moore, S.M., Pérez-Méndez, C., & Boerger, K,(2006) Meeting the needs of culturally and linguistically diverse families in early language and literacy intervention. In L. Justice (Ed.), *Clinical approaches to emergent literacy intervention* (pp. 29–70). San Diego, CA: Plural.

Muscott, H. S. (2002). Exceptional partnerships: Listening to the voices of families. *Preventing School Failure, 46*(2), 66–69.

National Center for Education Statistics. (2000). *The condition of education.* Washington, DC: U.S. Department of Education.

National Institute of Child Health and Human Development, National Institutes of Health, U.S. Department of Health and Human Services. (2006, January). *The NICHD study of early child care and youth development* (NIH Pub. No. 05-4318). Bethesda, MD: Author.

National Professional Development Center on Inclusion. (2007). *Recommendations for meaningfully involving families in state planning meetings.* Retrieved July 7, 2007, from http://www.fpg.unc.edu/~npdci/products.cfm

Oser, C., & Ayankoya, B. (2000). The early interventionist. *Zero to Three, 21*(2), 24–31.

Parental Information and Resource Centers. (2007). Retrieved January 23, 2007, from http://www.ed.gov/programs/pirc

Parette, H. P., & Brotherson, M. J. (2004). Family-centered and culturally responsive assistive technology decision-making. *Infants and Young Children, 17*(4), 355–367.

Park, J., & Turnbull, A. P. (2001). Cross cultural competence and special education: Perceptions and experiences of Korean parents of children with special needs. *Education and Training in Mental Retardation and Developmental Disabilities, 36*(2), 133–147.

Park, J., Turnbull, A. P., & Turnbull, H. R. (2002). Impacts of poverty on quality of life in families of children with disability. *Exceptional Children, 68*(2), 151–170.

Santelli, B., Poyadue, F. S., & Young, J. L. (2001). *The parent to parent handbook: Connecting families of children with special needs.* Baltimore: Brookes.

Schumacher, R. (2003). *Family support and parent involvement in Head Start: What do Head Start program performance standards require?* Washington, DC: Center for Law and Social Policy. Retrieved February 24, 2006, from http://www.clasp.org

Shelton, T. L., & Stepanek, J. S. (1994). *Family-centered care for children needing specialized health and developmental services.* Bethesda, MD: Association for the Care of Children's Health.

Shonkoff, J. P., & Phillips, D. A. (2000). *From neurons to neighborhoods: The science of early childhood development.* Washington, DC: National Academy Press.

Summers, J. A., Templeton-McMann, O., & Fuger, K. (1997). Critical thinking: A method to guide staff in serving families with multiple challenges. *Topics in Early Childhood Special Education, 17*(2), 27–52.

Technical Assistance Alliance for Parent Centers. (2006). Retrieved February 24, 2006, from http://www.taalliance.org/centers.

Thorp, E., & Sánchez, S. (in press). Infusing cultural and linguistic diversity into preservice and inservice preparation. In P. Winton, J. McCollum, & C. Catlett (Eds.), *Preparing effective professionals: Evidence and applications in early childhood and early intervention.* Washington, DC: Zero to Three.

Trivette, C. M., & Dunst, C. J. (2005). DEC recommended practices: Family-based practices. In S. Sandall, M. L. Hemmeter, B. J. Smith, & M. E. McLean (Eds.), *DEC recommended practices: A comprehensive guide for practical application in early intervention/early childhood special education* (pp. 107–126). Longmont, CO: Sopris West.

Turnbull, A. P., Blue-Banning, M., Turbiville, V., & Park, J. (1999). From parent education to partnership education: A call for a transformed focus. *Topics in Early Childhood Special Education, 19*(3), 164–171.

Turnbull, A. P., Summers, J. A., & Brotherson, M. J. (1984). *Working with families with disabled members: A family systems approach.* Lawrence: University of Kansas, Kansas Affiliated Facility.

Turnbull, A. P., Summers, J. A., Turnbull, R., Brotherson, M. J., Winton, P. J., Roberts, R., et al. (in press). Family supports and services in early childhood: A bold vision. *Journal of Early Childhood.*

Turnbull, A. P., Turnbull, R., Erwin, E., & Soodak, L. (2006). *Families, professionals, and exceptionality: Positive outcomes through partnership and trust* (5th ed.). Upper Saddle River, NJ: Merrill Prentice Hall.

U.S. Census Bureau. (2005). *2005 American community survey data.* Retrieved November 6, 2006, from http://factfinder.census.gov/servlet/ACSSAFFPeople?_submenuId=people_10&_sse=on

Wesley, P. W., & Buysse, V. (2001). Communities of practice: Expanding professional roles to promote reflection and shared inquiry. *Topics in Early Childhood Special Education, 21*, 114–124.

Winton, P. (1988). Effective communication between parents and professionals. In D. Bailey & R. Simeonsson (Eds.), *Family assessment in early intervention* (pp. 207–228). Columbus, OH: Merrill.

Winton, P. (1996). Understanding family concerns, priorities, and resources. In P. J. McWilliam, P. J. Winton, & E. Crais (Eds.), *Practical strategies for family-centered early intervention* (pp. 31–54). San Diego, CA: Singular Publishing.

Winton, P. (2000). Early childhood intervention personnel preparation: Backward mapping for future planning. *Topics in Early Childhood Special Education, 20*(2), 87–94.

Winton, P. (2006). The evidence-based practice movement and its effect on knowledge utilization. In V. Buysse & P. Wesley (Eds.), *Evidence-based practice in the early childhood field* (pp. 71–115). Washington, DC: Zero to Three.

Winton, P., & Turnbull, A. (1981). Parent involvement as viewed by parents of handicapped children. *Topics in Early Childhood Special Education, 1*(3), 11–20.

Winton, P., & Winton, R. (2005). Family systems. In J. Solomon (Ed.), *Pediatric skills for occupational therapy assistants* (2nd ed., pp. 11–22). St. Louis, MO: Mosby.

CHAPTER 3

FAMILY PARTNERSHIPS IN EARLY CHILDHOOD PROGRAMS

Don't Forget Fathers/Men

Brent A. McBride, Wm. Justin Dyer, and Thomas R. Rane

In recent years researchers, policymakers, and practitioners alike have witnessed a heightened interest in the roles of fathers and the concept of fatherhood (Marsiglio, Amato, Day, & Lamb, 2000). Evidence of this can be seen in the increased number of books, special issues of scholarly journals, and magazine articles that are devoted to this topic (e.g., Day & Lamb, 2004; Hawkins & Dollahite, 1997; Lamb, 2004; Tamis-LeMonda & Cabrera, 2002). Paralleling this increased attention has been a shift in societal expectations for fatherhood. These new societal expectations are calling for men to assume a more active role in raising their young children (Coltrane & Allan, 1994; Furstenberg, 1995; McBride, Rane, & Bae, 2001). The popular media treatment of this idea has gone so far as to suggest that "America is in the midst of an unprecedented revolution in men's paternal role expectations—that popular attitudes about what fathers can and should do

Promising Practices for Partnering with Families in the Early Years, pages 41–58
Copyright © 2008 by Information Age Publishing
All rights of reproduction in any form reserved.

are changing in ways not dreamed of before" (LaRossa, Gordon, Wilson, Bauran, & Jaret, 1991, p. 994).

At the same time this shift in societal expectations for fathers has occurred, a renewed interest in the roles that family members play in the educational process for their children has emerged. A growing theoretical and empirical literature base suggests that active family partnerships in elementary and early childhood settings can have a positive impact on child outcomes (e.g., Epstein & Sanders, 2002; Fagan & Palm, 2004; Powell, 1993). A significant body of research indicates that when families participate in their children's education the result is an improvement in student achievement and student attitudes (Walker et al., 2004). Increased school attendance, fewer discipline problems, and higher aspirations also have been linked to parent involvement and family–school partnerships (Epstein & Sanders, 2002; Hill et al., 2004). Studies also document that when families are involved in school, they gain a clearer understanding of what is expected of their children and how they can work with their children and teachers to enhance their children's educational experience (Epstein & Sanders, 2002).

One important but often overlooked focus in the effort to increase family–school partnerships in elementary and early childhood programs, however, is the involvement of fathers (McBride et al., 2001). While the term "family" is often used by researchers, teachers, and policymakers alike when discussing "family–school partnerships," most efforts that focus on such partnerships often fail to include the father of the child. For example, a 2004 review of over 1,000 recent articles in the four leading U.S. school psychology journals found that fathers were included substantially in only nine articles, and were the primary focus of just one (Grief & Grief, 2004). However, there is a growing research base that points to just how important fathers are as a resource.

BENEFITS OF FATHER INVOLVEMENT

Numerous studies have shown that when men assume active roles in raising their children, they play a critical part in enhancing and facilitating child growth and development (see Pleck & Masciadrelli, 2004, for a review). For example, recent research has suggested that both the quantity and quality of father–child interactions during the early childhood years can lead to more positive social development (Frosch, Cox, & Goldman, 2001), fewer behavioral problems (Jaffee, Moffitt, Caspi, & Taylor, 2003), greater emotional self-regulation (Roggman, Boyce, Cook, Christiansen, & Jones, 2004), increased language development (Magill-Evans & Harrison, 2001), and greater cognitive functioning (Gauvain, Fagot, Lee, & Kavanagh, 2002) for young children.

The potential benefits of increased father involvement extend beyond the context of the home environment. Recent research has identified multiple positive linkages between father involvement and children's growth and development when men become engaged in home–school partnership activities. These positive linkages are independent of the impact of mothers' involvement (Fagan & Inglesias, 1999; Flouri, 2005; Flouri & Buchanan, 2004; McBride, Schoppe-Sullivan, & Ho, 2005; National Center for Education Statistics, 1998b; U.S. Department of Education, 2000). For example, data drawn from the National Center for Education Statistics' (NCES) 1996 National Household Education Survey (NCES, 1998b) suggests that children whose fathers are involved in their schooling (regardless of whether their fathers live with them) are half as likely to ever repeat a grade and are significantly less likely to ever be suspended or expelled. Even after taking into account mothers' involvement, fathers' and mothers' education, household income, and children's race/ethnicity, children with fathers who were highly involved were more likely to get A's, participate in extracurricular activities, and to enjoy school. Nord and West (2001) found that these same positive linkages between father involvement and academic performance persisted across a variety of family types (e.g., families with two biological parents, stepfather families, and fathers heading single-parent families).

Both fathers and programs also benefit when men become involved in home–program partnership activities. Hawkins and Dollahite (1997) call attention to benefits that fathers derive when they become involved with their children. As fathers do the "work" of fathering (Hawkins & Dollahite, 1997) it can initiate/facilitate growth in maturity, social skills, and personal responsibility. The more fathers are able to be involved in their children's programs, the more effective that involvement becomes. Involvement is also beneficial to the father as it tends to build fathers' connections to the larger community. Thus, families, early childhood programs, and society subsequently benefit from these increased abilities.

POTENTIAL BARRIERS

While the above findings are very encouraging for programs attempting to involve fathers/men, there are many forces that work against achieving this goal, both on the side of families and program staff. Understanding these forces assists in determining ways to move forward and build partnerships that include fathers/men.

Epstein's Life-Course Perspective of Home–School Partnerships

Epstein's (1987) life-course perspective of home–school partnerships has proven to be beneficial as researchers and educators attempt to identify potential barriers to effective family involvement strategies in early childhood programs. This model, shown in Figure 3.1, suggests that the degree of overlap between home and school environments (i.e., home–school partnerships) is controlled by three forces. Force A refers to both individual and historical time—that is, the age of the child and the extant sociocultural conditions at the point the child enrolls in a particular early childhood program. Force B and Force C refer to the prior experiences and philosophies of families and schools. These two forces will either push together or pull apart home–school partnerships. For example, a family that has had positive experiences with early childhood programs and places a high value on education will put an emphasis on increasing the amount of overlap between home and school environments. Taken together, these three forces combine to play a critical role in determining how, and the extent to which, home–school partnerships develop within early childhood programs.

Epstein's (1987) model also provides an effective tool for identifying those factors that may limit and/or discourage fathers from becoming involved in early childhood programs. As mentioned earlier, a shift has occurred in recent years in societal expectations for paternal roles (Force A in Epstein's model). Although this shift in societal expectations has filtered down to early childhood settings, for a variety of reasons many men are reluctant and/or are uncomfortable in becoming involved in early childhood settings (Force B). At the same time, the majority of early childhood teachers are limited in their understanding of how to encourage fathers

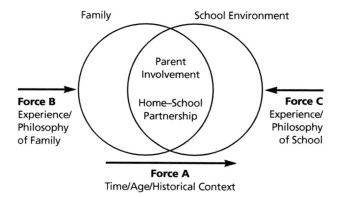

Figure 3.1 Epstein's (1987) model of overlapping spheres of influence between home and school environments.

to become involved with their programs (Force C) (McBride et al., 2001). As a result, many educators (and fathers as well) are reluctant, and even resistant to, expanding family–partnership activities in early childhood programs to include fathers/men.

There are several forces that work against family partnerships both on the side of families and program staff (Force B and Force C in Epstein's model). For instance, NCES (1998a) found that parents' lack of time and negative attitudes toward the school were significant barriers to family partnerships (Force B). NCES also found similar barriers for school staff including a lack of time, lack of staff training in working with families, and staff members' negative attitudes toward family involvement (Force C). Furthermore, several studies have found that family involvement in general is more problematic for families with lower socioeconomic status (Comer, 1988; McBride et al., 2001; Powell, 1993; Reynolds, 1992). These problems often include socioeconomic differences between families and staff, as well as families' lack of understanding on how to help with their children's schoolwork (Force B and Force C). Minority families also encounter further difficulties as a result of potential language barriers and cultural differences between families and staff (NCES, 1998a).

In addition to the above barriers, recent research (e.g., Fagan & Palm, 2004; Gavazzi & Schock, 2004) indicates that men often face many challenges in family-centered early childhood programs. For instance, fathers are less likely to be involved in early childhood programs because of conflicts with work schedules (Force B). Similarly, many fathers also fail to become involved in these programs due to feelings of low confidence in their own parenting abilities (Force B). Some fathers report they do not participate in programs because they are never informed of family involvement opportunities, an especially problematic issue for nonresident fathers (Force C). Finally, fathers often do not participate in early childhood programs because of the gendered nature of such settings (Force C).

Misconceptions and Myths

Educators' reluctance to involve fathers may in part be due to misconceptions about fathers' involvement with their children. The notion that most children, particularly those from low-income and high-risk backgrounds, have little contact with their fathers is a myth that permeates program development efforts. In addition, Fagan (1994) found that many early childhood teachers hold the belief that fathers are not interested in volunteering in the classroom and that they do not like to work with children. Myths such as these have had a significant negative impact on policies and practices designed to encourage the participation of fathers and men in partnership initiatives in early childhood programs.

Emerging research has begun to challenge many of the myths that have served as barriers to fathers becoming involved in early childhood programs. First, while fathers' involvement is, on average, much less than mothers', numerous studies have documented an increase in paternal involvement across a variety of contexts (see Pleck & Mascidrelli, 2004, for a review). Currently, researchers are observing a change in the "rhythms" of family life (Bianchi, Robinson, & Milkie, 2006), noting that amid the changes in family life over the past few decades fathers have "responded by increasing their domestic hours, first in housework, and more recently in child care… not only in the United States but elsewhere" (p. 177). This increase has been both in absolute terms (i.e., number of hours per day involved) as well as relative terms (i.e., in comparison with mothers' involvement).

Second, while there has been little research regarding father's attitudes toward involvement in early childhood programs, the few studies that have been conducted are encouraging (Fagan & Palm, 2004). For example, Turbiville, Umbarger, and Guthrie (2000) found that fathers expressed interest in being involved in their children's programs. This included fathers with children in child care centers, Head Start programs, and programs for infants, toddlers, and preschoolers with disabilities. Similarly, in Hadadian and Merbler's (1995) study of 201 fathers of children with disabilities, 84 percent of fathers said that they probably would participate in activities designed for their children.

Unfortunately, myths such as those mentioned above have restricted initiatives designed to encourage father involvement in early childhood programs and home settings, a restriction that results in lost opportunities for administrators and early childhood educators to acknowledge and build upon the strengths that many men bring to the parenting situation— strengths that can be utilized in the building of more effective family partnerships (Levine, 1993; McBride & Rane, 1997). Indeed, as Pruett (2000) remarked, "Men are the single greatest untapped resource in the lives of American children" (p. 217).

ENCOURAGING FATHER INVOLVMENT IN EARLY CHILDHOOD PROGRAMS

The creation of family involvement and support programs designed specifically for fathers may be one way to help early childhood educators to understand the importance of father involvement and to effectively establish partnerships with fathers within the framework of their programs (Fagan & Iglesias, 1999). Such initiatives can also expand the range of support services early childhood programs are able to offer as they attempt to facilitate family partnerships. One important question concerns the effectiveness of interventions designed to increase partnerships between fathers and early childhood programs. Below we report on the impact of an intervention created to train early childhood educators on how to involve fathers and men in their programs (see McBride et al., 2001, for a more detailed discussion of the project). We briefly outline this intervention project and report results of an evaluation. Finally, we offer insights on improving partnerships between fathers and early childhood programs.

Father/Male Involvement Intervention Program

The target site for implementing the intervention program was a large, state-funded pre-kindergarten (PreK) "at-risk" program in Illinois. Based on pilot work conducted for this current project, an "indirect" intervention program was developed and implemented. The purpose of this indirect intervention was to provide 3 years of support services to teachers working in the target PreK program in order to allow them to develop the knowledge base required to successfully plan, implement, and evaluate specific father/male involvement initiatives. The nature and content of activities implemented as part of the indirect intervention covered a broad spectrum, including staff development training sessions, sponsorship of special men's and kids' events (e.g., gym night, field trip to the bowling alley), consultation meetings with individual teachers on issues related to father involvement (e.g., how to engage a father in conversations about his child's behavioral problems), outreach initiatives to families of enrolled children on issues related to father involvement (e.g., newsletter to enrolled families publicizing events), and facilitation of team meeting discussions on father involvement and parent involvement in general. The focus of the intervention was flexible enough to meet the needs of the teachers at whatever comfort level and knowledge base they found themselves in relation to father involvement.

Basic Assumptions and Values for Promoting Father/Male Involvement

In developing and implementing the indirect intervention, the program development group focused on four specific issues identified by McBride and Rane (1997) as being critical to the success of initiatives designed to encourage father/male involvement in early childhood programs. First, the intervention program was developed under the premise that not all staff members would be equally committed to the concept of father involvement. Thus, the program included activities (e.g., father involvement self-reflection inventories) to allow teachers the opportunity to address, discuss, and explore their concerns and biases against such efforts. Second, the program development group created clearly articulated rationales for why their program and classrooms should be concerned about facilitating father/male involvement. Third, the program development group worked with the teams of teachers to clearly specify the targets of their initiatives. Working with the school social workers, teachers identified the various men they were aware of who had some form of regular involvement with children enrolled in their classrooms. It was acknowledged by all teachers that most children enrolled had some sort of consistent interaction with a male. Thus, all efforts implemented as part of this initiative targeted fathers of enrolled children, or the "significant" male figure for these children.

Finally, like most PreK programs, the program that was given the intervention already had in place a wide range of initiatives designed to encourage parent involvement, although targeted primarily at mothers. With the help of a data collection tool designed specifically for this project, each team of teachers was continuously encouraged to examine their efforts to facilitate parent involvement and family–school partnership activities, and to explore how these initiatives could be adapted to better meet the needs of fathers/men. With such an emphasis, the teachers were not being asked to start from the beginning in their efforts to establish partnerships with fathers/men.

Intervention Program Evaluation

In order to evaluate the effectiveness of the intervention initiative, family–school partnership activities at the school in which teachers received father involvement training (see McBride & Rane, 1997, for more detail about the father involvement training program) was then compared to a school where teachers did not receive this training. All teachers (at both schools that received the intervention and those that did not) participated in data collection procedures in order to evaluate the intervention program. Evaluation data were collected during the third year of the intervention program. At the beginning of the academic year teachers completed a packet of questionnaires that included questions about their educational backgrounds, their attitudes toward father involvement, and their general attitudes toward parent involvement. During the school year teachers also logged information about each contact they had with family members. This log included information about phone calls, school visits, home visits, and other types of family–school partnership contacts. Also included in this log was information about the nature/focus of the contact. For example, for each contact it was noted whether the teacher and family discussed the child's developmental progress, the child's behavior, the child's health issues, etc. It was also noted whether it was the school or the family who initiated the contact.

Evaluation Outcomes

Results of our evaluation indicated that those teachers who received the intervention were more likely to have fathers/males initiate contact with the school than those teachers who did not receive the intervention (see McBride et al., 2001, for a full report on the evaluation study). The findings also indicated that the intervention resulted in more joint father–mother contacts. Results also indicated that teachers at the intervention site reported a significantly higher proportion of their family–school partnership contacts were with fathers/males than those of the nonintervention site teachers. Conversely, teachers at the nonintervention site reported that a significantly higher proportion of their family involvement contacts were with females than those of intervention site teachers. These findings indicate that teachers at the intervention site were experiencing greater levels of participation in parent involvement and family–school partnership activities across the various categories with fathers/men than teachers at the nonintervention site.

Due to several limitations that are present in the design used to evaluate this initiative (e.g., lack of long-term follow-up and small sample size), caution must be used in generalizing results to other similar intervention programs. However, the results of this evaluation are encouraging for continued research and program development work in this area. Findings suggested that fathers/men at the intervention site program were participating in parent involvement and family–school partnership activities at a significantly higher rate than that reported at the nonintervention site program. In addition, family involvement contacts that were home initiated were done so at a significantly higher rate by fathers/men affiliated with the treatment site program than those home-initiated contacts at the control site program. The indirect intervention program provides a promising model of support services that may be instrumental in helping early childhood educators identify ways to encourage and facilitate father involvement in their programs. Initiatives with an empirical basis such as this are significantly strengthened in their effectiveness, and have an increased ability for continued growth and improvement (McBride & Lutz, 2004).

RECOMMENDED PRACTICES
IN EARLY CHILDHOOD PROGRAMS

In addition to the evaluative data that highlights the positive impact of the program developed, process data collected over the 3 years of implementing this indirect intervention provide insight into several issues that should be addressed if similar programs are to be successful. Early childhood practitioners and parent educators can use these insights as starting points or as suggestions for how to begin exploring ways in which to encourage more father participation in family–school partnership initiatives in their programs.

Formulate a Clear Rationale

Early childhood educators will need to build a strong rationale for developing father–program partnership initiatives. Educators need to be specific in their reasons for developing family–partnership initiatives targeted at fathers/men. Prior to developing specific initiatives, educators must ask themselves why they think such efforts are important, and how the initiatives could enhance the services being provided to children and families. Fagan and Palm (2004) have outlined a clearly articulated overview of the benefits to encouraging father–program partnerships in early childhood settings. These benefits, some of which have been highlighted in this chapter (see the section "Benefits of Father Involvement," above), must be the focus of the rationale for reaching out to men. Focusing on father–program partnerships simply because it is currently a "hot" societal issue increases the likelihood that such efforts will wane when the next big issue emerges.

Acknowledge Resistance

Early childhood educators must acknowledge that not everyone will be committed to the concept of parent involvement and family–school partnership initiatives targeted at fathers/men. Many people will question why resources should be targeted at fathers/men when they are viewed as the primary cause of the problems facing children. The experience of this intervention showed that resistance will come from teachers, school administrators, community leaders, mothers, and men themselves. While the evaluation did find that teachers in general had positive attitudes about father involvement, resistance to the intervention initiatives was expressed by some teachers at the treatment site, indicating a possible social desirability in their responses on this measure. Program developers must recognize that such resistance may occur in spite of teachers' reports that they are in favor of father/male involvement and partnerships. However, acquiring an understanding of the benefits of father involvement may help to minimize resistance.

Clearly Specify Targets

Educators also need to be specific about the targets of their efforts to encourage father–school partnership. Research data has indicated that many children growing up in low-income and single-parent homes have regular and consistent interactions with a father and/or male role figure, although not necessarily their biological father (Levine, 1993). Focusing efforts exclusively on biological fathers will exclude a large proportion of men who play significant roles in the lives of these children. The key for educators will be to identify which men in the lives of children can be effectively targeted for partnership effort. One simple step to gather this information would be to include questions regarding the men in children's lives as part of the intake/enrollment process.

Do Not Reinvent the Wheel

Many early childhood programs already include comprehensive family–partnership components, although they tend to be targeted primarily at mothers. When developing initiatives for father–program partnerships, program leaders should first evaluate the family involvement components already in place and explore how they may be adapted to reach out to men in order to meet their unique needs. For example, if a program currently has in place a training session to prepare volunteers (primarily mothers/women) for working in classrooms, they should consider creating a parallel session for fathers/men that would focus on helping men become more comfortable participating in early childhood settings.

Help Women Become Facilitators

Although it would be desirable to have a male staff member provide leadership to such initiatives, this is often not possible because the majority of professionals in the field are females. Of course women can provide effective leadership in these outreach efforts, but to be successful they must be knowledgeable of and sensitive to differences in the ways men and women approach parenting and interact with young children. Men bring a unique set of strengths and needs to the parenting realm (McBride, 1990). The ways in which they have been socialized while growing up has contributed to differences in their communication styles, thought processes, expression of feelings, and so on, compared to women (Fagan & Palm, 2004). These differences need to be understood in the context of program services designed to facilitate and encourage father–program partnerships in early childhood programs. As Palm and Johnson (1992) have argued, it is not the intention that acknowledgment of these differences will be used to reinforce negative sex-role stereotypes, but that denying differences in parenting styles limits the ability of programs to identify and address men's unique needs. Female leaders of outreach efforts to fathers/men must acknowledge these differences and build upon the strengths men bring to the table while at the same time being sensitive to men's needs.

Involve Mothers in Developing Initiatives

From the very beginning mothers need to be involved in the development of initiatives designed to encourage father–program partnerships. They need to be made aware of both why resources are being put into developing these activities and how they and their children will benefit. Mothers tend to be the gatekeepers for access to their children (McBride et al., 2005), especially with noncustodial fathers and significant male role figures (Fagan & Barnett, 2003). Eliciting the support and involvement of mothers in developing such initiatives can provide access to fathers/men and help ensure the success of these programs (i.e., women involved in developing these initiatives are more likely to encourage men in the lives of their children to participate in the programs).

Continue to Meet Mothers' Needs

As early childhood educators develop initiatives to encourage father–program partnerships, they must not do so at the expense of efforts targeted at mothers. Acknowledging the unique strengths and needs of fathers/men underscores the point that mothers also have unique contributions to make to their children's progress and success in school settings. While establishing initiatives to reach out to men, ongoing consistent efforts to partner with mothers must be maintained.

Create a Climate for Father/Male Involvement

One key to success for these efforts lies in building a father-/male-friendly environment that facilitates a culture of male involvement in the program (e.g., creating an information bulletin board specifically for fathers/men, having a clearly identified adult male restroom in what is typically a female- and child-dominated environment). Creating a climate of partnerships with fathers/men is a long-term process. In building such a climate, men will begin to feel a sense of acceptance in terms of their participation and the importance of the roles they can play within the program, and also an expectation on the part of the program that men should assume more active roles.

Acknowledge Diversity in Family Structure

When trying to facilitate and encourage more father/male participation in family–program partnership activities, it is critical to acknowledge the diversity of family situations and that father–child and father–family relationships may be very complex (Marsiglio et al., 2000). Particular issues may come up when working with nonresident fathers (Fagan & Palm, 2004). For example, nonresident fathers often have a contentious relationship with mothers that may influence them to be more disconnected with their childs' programs.

When interacting with mothers, sensitivity is required when broaching the subject of a nonresident father's involvement. While mothers who have difficult relationships with the fathers may be initially resistant to father involvement, they may begin to open up (perhaps not right away) to the possibility if staff describe the benefits of paternal involvement. Of course, valid reasons for a father's noninvolvement exist (history of abuse, etc.) and staff should not push for involvement once the mother's position is made clear. However, when fathers with contentious mother relationships are involved, staff can facilitate (without allying themselves with either parent against the other) a level of father involvement that each parent feels is fair (see Fagan & Palm, 2004, for an extended overview of this issue).

Proceed Slowly

Efforts to build a culture of father/male involvement and partnerships are much more likely to succeed if educators begin working with men in their comfort zone. Most men have not spent extended periods of time in early childhood classrooms and may thus feel unprepared to actively participate in this environment. Don't expect too much too soon. Start slow and build upon successes. Initially, it may be important to give men choices of activities, finding out from each what contribution they would feel comfortable making.

Provide Training and Support Services

Most staff of early childhood programs receive little, if any, formalized education or training in the area of parent involvement and family–program partnerships. This is especially true in the area of father/male involvement in early childhood programs. If such efforts are to be successful, early childhood educators will need to be provided with ongoing development and in-service training experiences that give them a knowledge base from which to design and implement specific initiatives to encourage father/male involvement in their programs.

Evaluate Efforts

For many practitioners engaged in the development and implementation of initiatives to encourage father participation in parent involvement and family–school partnership activities, the concept of program evaluation is often viewed as an ominous process that is better left in the hands of university researchers, and one that has little relevance to what they are trying to achieve in their programs. As a result of this lack of emphasis on evaluation, many of these initiatives suffer from the same types of problems (e.g., lack of shared resources, lack of a common knowledge base on how to develop initiatives for fathers and men, a "trial and error" approach to developing new initiatives focusing on fathers, etc.). The failure to place an emphasis on evaluating efforts has limited the dissemination and replication of programs for fathers that have been successful in local early childhood programs, and restricts the potential success that many locally developed initiatives are able to achieve.

Program evaluation should be viewed as the systematic collection and analysis of program-related data that can be used to understand how a program delivers services and/or what the consequences of its services are for participants (Jacobs, 1988). Several program evaluation models are available that can be used to guide efforts that focus on fathers. For example, the *Fathering Indicators Framework* developed by Gadsden, Fagan, Ray, and Davis (2001) provides an effective paradigm that can guide practitioners in exploring how evaluation can become a core component of their efforts to encourage father participation in family–school partnership activities.

CONCLUSION

While involving fathers in early childhood programs has only recently received attention in practice and research, these experiences and studies have evidenced benefits (to both children and fathers) when fathers are involved. Clearly, this is not intended as an exhaustive list of recommendations related to the successful development and implementation of specific initiatives to increase father–school partnerships in early childhood programs. Nonetheless, based on recent research and our own experiences in developing and evaluating the intervention program described in this chapter, the recommendations presented here form a helpful framework for beginning the important task of developing and implementing initiatives to increase partnerships with fathers in early childhood programs.

REFERENCES

Bianchi, S. M., Robinson, J. P., & Milkie, M. A. (2006). *Changing rhythms of American family life.* New York: Russell Sage Foundation.

Coltrane, S., & Allan, K. (1994). "New" fathers and old stereotypes: Representations of masculinity in 1980's television advertising. *Masculinities, 2,* 1–25.

Comer, J.P. (1988). Educating poor minority children. *Scientific American, 259,* 42–48.

Day, R. D., & Lamb, M. E. (2004). *Conceptualizing and measuring father involvement.* Mahwah, NJ: Erlbaum.

Epstein, J. L. (1987). Toward a theory of family–school connections: Teacher practices and parent involvement. In K. Hurrelman, F. Kaufmann & F. Losel (Eds.), *Social intervention: Potential and constraints* (pp. 121–136). New York: Aldine de Gruyter.

Epstein, J. L., & Sanders, M. G. (2002). Family, school, and community partnerships. In M. H. Bornstein (Ed.), *Handbook of parenting* (2nd ed., Vol. 5, pp. 407–437). Mahwah, NJ: Erlbaum.

Fagan, J. (1994). Evaluation of the Philadelphia Parent Child Center's Men's Involvement Program. Philadelphia: Author.

Fagan, J., & Barnett, M. (2003). The relationship between maternal gatekeeping, paternal competence, mothers' attitudes about the father role, and father involvement. *Journal of Family Issues, 24*(8), 1020–1043.

Fagan, J., & Palm, G. (2004). *Fathers and early childhood programs.* Clifton Park, NY: Delmar.

Fagan, J., & Inglesias, A. (1999). Father involvement program effects on fathers, father figures, and their Head Start children: A quasi-experimental study. *Early Childhood Research Quarterly, 14*(2), 243–269.

Flouri, E. (2005). *Fathering and child outcomes.* West Sussex, UK: Wiley.

Flouri, E., & Buchanan, A. (2004). Early father's and mother's involvement and child's later educational outcomes. *British Journal of Educational Psychology, 74,* 141–153.

Furstenburg, F.F., Jr. (1995). Fathering in the inner city: Paternal participation and public policy. In W. Marsiglio (Ed.), *Fatherhood: Contemporary theory, research, and social policy* (pp. 41–56). Thousand Oaks, CA: Sage.

Frosch, C. A., Cox, M. J, & Goldman, B. D. (2001). Infant-parent attachment and parental child behavior during parent–toddler storybook interaction. *Merrill–Palmer Quarterly, 47,* 445–474.

Gadsden, V., Fagan, J., Ray, A., & Davis, J.E. (2001). *The Fathering Indicators Framework: A tool for quantitative and qualitative analysis.* Retrieved from the National Center on Fathers and Families website at http://www.ncof.gse.upenn.edu

Gavazzi, S., & Schock, A. (2004). A multimethod study of father participation in family-based programming. In R. D. Day & M. E. Lamb (Eds.), *Conceptualizing and measuring father involvement* (pp. 149–184). Mahwah, NJ: Erlbaum.

Gauvain, M., Fagot, B. I., Leve, C., & Kavanagh, K. (2002). Instruction by mothers and fathers during problem solving with their young children. *Journal of Family Psychology, 16,* 81–90.

Greif, J. L., & Greif, G. L. (2004). Including fathers in school psychology literature: A review of four school psychology journals. *Psychology in the Schools, 41*(5), 575–580.

Hadadian, A., & Merbler, J. (1995). Fathers of young children with disabilities: How do they want to be involved? *Child and Youth Care Forum, 24,* 327–338.

Hawkins, A. J., & Dollahite, D. C. (1997). *Generative fathering: Beyond deficit perspectives.* Thousand Oaks, CA: Sage.

Hill, N. E., Castellino, D. R., Lansford, J. E., Nowlin, P., Dodge, K. A., Bates, J. E., et al. (2004). Parent academic involvement as related to school behavior, achievement, and aspirations: Demographic variations across adolescence. *Child Development, 75,* 1491–1509.

Jacobs, F. H. (1988). The five tiered approach to evaluation: Context and implementation. In H. B. Weiss & F. H. Jacobs (Eds.), *Evaluating Family Programs* (pp. 37–68). New York: Aldine de Gruyter.

Jaffee, S. R., Moffitt, T. E., Caspi, A., & Taylor, A. (2003). Life with (or without) father: The benefits of living with two biological parents depend on the father's antisocial behavior. *Child Development, 74,* 109–126.

Lamb, M. E. (2004). *The role of the father in child development* (4th ed.). New York: Wiley.

LaRossa, R., Gordon, R.J., Wilson, A., Bauran, A., & Jaret, C. (1991). The fluctuating image of the 20th century American father. *Journal of Marriage and the Family, 53,* 987–997.

Levine, J. A. (1993). Involving fathers in Head Start: A framework for public policy and program development. *Families in Society, 74,* 4–19.

Magill-Evans, J., & Harrison, M.J. (2001). Parent-child interactions, parenting stress, and developmental outcomes at 4 years. *Children's Health Care, 30,* 135–150.

Marsiglio, W., Amato, P., Day, R. D., & Lamb, M. E. (2000). Scholarship on fatherhood in the 1990s and beyond. *Journal of Marriage and Family, 62*(4), 1173–1191.

McBride, B. A. (1990). The effects of a parent education/play group program on father involvement. *Family Relations, 39,* 250–256.

McBride, B. A., Brown, G. L., Bost, K. K., Shin, N., Vaughn, B., & Korth, B. (2005). Paternal identity, maternal gatekeeping, and father involvement. *Family Relations, 54,* 360–372.

McBride, B. A., & Lutz, M. M. (2004). Intervention: Changing the nature and extent of father involvement. In M. E. Lamb (Ed.), *The role of the father in child development* (4th ed., pp. 446-475). New York: Wiley.

McBride, B. A., & Rane, T. R. (1997). Father involvement in early childhood programs: Issues and challenges. *Early Childhood Education Journal, 25,* 11–15.

McBride, B. A., Rane, T. R., & Bae, J. (2001). Father/male involvement in prekindergarten at-risk programs: An exploratory study. *Early Childhood Research Quarterly, 16,* 77–93.

McBride, B. A., Schoppe-Sullivan, S. J., & Ho, M. (2005). The mediating role of fathers' school involvement on student achievement. *Journal of Applied Developmental Psychology, 26,* 201–216.

National Center for Education Statistics. (1998b). *Students do better when their fathers are involved at school.* Available at http://nces.ed.gov/web/pubs98/98121.asp

National Center for Education Statistics. (1998a). *Parent involvement in children's education: Efforts by public elementary schools.* Available at http://nces.ed.gov/pubs98/98032.pdf

Nord, C. W., & West, J. (2001). Fathers' and mothers' involvement in their children's schools by family type and resident status. *Education Statistics Quarterly, 3.* Retrieved December 11, 2006, from http://nces.ed.gov/pubsearch/pubsinfo.asp?pubid=98121

Palm, G., & Johnson, L. (1992). *Working with fathers: Methods and perspectives.* Stillwater, MN: Nu Ink Unlimited.

Pleck, J. H., & Masciadrelli, B. P. (2004). Paternal involvement by U.S. resident fathers: Levels, sources, and consequences. In M. E. Lamb (Ed.), *The role of the father in child development* (4th ed., pp. 222-271). New York: Wiley.

Powell, D. R. (1993). Supporting parent–child relationships in the early years: Lessons learned and yet to be learned. In T. H. Brubaker (Ed.), *Family relations: Challenges for the future* (pp. 79–97). Newbury Park, CA: Sage.

Pruett, K. D. (2000). *Fatherneed: Why father care is as essential as mother care for your child.* New York: Free Press.

Reynolds, A. J. (1992). Comparing measures of parental involvement and their effects on academic achievement. *Early Childhood Research Quarterly, 7,* 441–462.

Roggman, L., Boyce, L., Cook, G., Christiansen, K., & Jones, D. (2004). Playing with Daddy: Social toy play, early head start, and developmental outcomes. *Fathering, 2,* 83–108.

Tamis-LeMonda, C. S., & Cabrera, N. (2002). *Handbook of father involvement: Multidisciplinary perspectives.* Mahwah, NJ: Erlbaum.

Turbiville, V. P., Umbarger, G. T., & Guthrie, A. C. (2000). Fathers' involvement in programs for young children. *Young Children, 55,* 74–79.

U.S. Department of Education. (2000). *A call to commitment: Fathers' involvement in children's learning.* Retrieved July 13, 2006, from http://www.ed.gov/pubs/parents/calltocommit/

Walker, J. M., Hover-Dembsey, K. V., Whetsel, D. R., & Green, C.L. (2004). *Parental involvement in homework: A review of current research and its implications for teachers, after school program staff, and parent leaders.* Cambridge, MA: Harvard Family Research Project.

CHAPTER 4

EASING THE TRANSITION

Family Support Programs and Early School Success

Billie Enz, Michelle Rhodes, and Marilyn LaCount

INTRODUCTION

Kindergarten was first developed to ease the transition into formal schooling by enhancing children's cognitive, physical, and social development
through nurturing child-centered, play-based experiences (Bloch, 1987; Pianta & Cox, 1999). Historically, kindergarten was a time for children to develop their own unique skills through social interactions with others (Bryant & Clifford, 1992). Sadly, over the last two decades, American society has
placed heavy academic demands on its young children. Children are now
required to begin school with phonemic awareness, knowledge of letters
and sounds, and early numeracy skills that once had been the curriculum
of kindergarten (National Education Panel, 1995). As the National Education Panel (1995) stated: "by the year 2000, all children will start school
ready to succeed." Hence, the emphasis of kindergarten has changed
significantly. The play-based, exploratory curriculum is fast fading as the
academic kindergarten of today is usually characterized by the direct in-

Promising Practices for Partnering with Families in the Early Years, pages 59–78
Copyright © 2008 by Information Age Publishing
All rights of reproduction in any form reserved.

59

struction of specific discrete skills, particularly in reading and math, which children are expected to master before going to first grade (Bracey, 2000; Egertson, 1987; Katz, Raths, & Torres, 1987). These high academic expectations are being reinforced nationally. Although some children enter the new kindergarten "ready to succeed," many others start school without the prerequisite knowledge (Elkind, 1986; Moyer, 1999; National Center for Early Development and Learning, 1998). The question now becomes, how can we help young children succeed in this new environment?

Research consistently states that parental and family involvement in young children's education has been found to have the greatest influence on children's initial and long-term success in school (Connell & Prinz, 2001; Logsdon, 1998; Henderson & Berla, 1994; Marcon, 1999; Seitz, Rosenbaum, & Apfel, 1985; Olmsted, 1991; Oden, Schweinhart, & Weikart, 2000; Schweinhart et al., 2005). Families who understand the school's curriculum and the school's expectations can support their young children's efforts by providing home activities that are school-like in nature. For example, parents can engage in games with their children that focus on looking for words that begin with specific letters, counting and categorizing household items, and reading bedtime stories in a way that encourages comprehension and vocabulary.

While families from all socioeconomic levels and ethnic backgrounds want their children to be successful in school, most have little understanding of what is now expected of young children in today's kindergarten classroom (Gonzalez et al., 2005; Piotrokowski, Botsko, & Matthews, 2001). Helping families to understand school requirements and expectations enables them to become effectively involved in their child's learning (Diamond, Reagan, & Bandyk, 2000; Enz, 2003). Therefore, early childhood educators need to consider how curricular information can be shared thoughtfully and respectfully with families.

Parent education programs can help strengthen and smooth the transition between home and kindergarten (Connell & Prinz, 2001; Enz, 2003; National Center for Early Development and Learning, 1998; Oden et al., 2000). Over the past 20 years, a variety of programs have been developed to assist families in their efforts to provide their young children with educational experiences that will prepare them to participate fully in kindergarten (Enz, Perry, & Yi, 2003). In this chapter we describe and examine eight exemplary programs and the contributions they have made in promoting children's early school success. First, we begin by discussing the readiness expectations for the new academic kindergarten. Then, we illustrate home activities that are most likely to help children make a successful transition to school. Next, we present three categories of parent education programs: Family Support Programs, Family Interactive Programs, and Traditional Parent Education Programs. We describe each briefly, explore their positive effects, and make recommendations based on their successes. Finally, we conclude with a brief examination of the importance of the "system ready" concept and receptive systems in providing high-quality family-support programs.

READY TO SUCCEED

What does it mean to be ready to succeed? The definition of success has changed greatly over the past 50 years. In the past, the concept of kindergarten readiness included much more than a child's academic knowledge and skills. It involved children's physical health, self-confidence, and social competence. It also referred to having knowledge of the social rules and etiquette of classroom behavior, and having self-help skills such as being able to tie one's shoes and button one's shirt (Ferguson, 2005).

In the past, readiness also had implications for schools and their teaching staff. Traditionally it referred to a kindergarten teacher's ability to work with and support all of the children's variations in maturation. It was the school's job to ensure that all children's individual needs were being met. Thus, schools were responsible for ensuring that they were ready for all the variations in children's individual differences (National Association for the Education of Young Children, 1995). In other words, in order to ensure children's success in school, two factors had to be considered: (1) a child's readiness to be successful and (2) the school system's readiness to support the child's development.

Today, more than ever before, children enter school with widely varying school-like experiences and skills. Some children have participated in experiences, such as preschool, while others have not participated in any school-like experiences outside of their homes. Some children may be able to recognize letters, numbers, shapes, and may even be able to spell their names, whereas others haven't begun these types of activities yet. But as kindergarten teachers and early childhood experts can verify, children's development is irregular and episodic. Although nearly all children will eventually accomplish the same developmental milestones, these skills are not attained at the exact same time or in the same order for every child (Cannella, 2002). Every child is unique and thus comes to school with different skills (Ackerman & Barnett, 2005).

In the 1940s and 1950s it was believed that teachers were able to bring each child up to a standard level of success. James Coleman (1966), however, was one of the first to revise the idea that children's success in school depended primarily on the teacher's knowledge, skills, and practices; instead, he argued (and research over the past 40 years continues to support) that a child's success in school also depends on what knowledge, language, and experiences the children bring from their homes. Research consistently demonstrates that children's academic achievement is consistently related to their socioeconomic levels, resulting in an "achievement gap." An "achievement gap" refers to the differences that exist between children who are ready for success in school and those who are not (Valdes, 1996). In many instances, children who are not ready for success in school tend to be economically disadvantaged, often children of color, and who are learning English as a second language (Valdes, 1996).

A child's background has been identified as such a significant influence in school achievement that families today are often blamed for a child's failure in school, especially language-minority families. When children have difficulties at school, oftentimes the school system blames families for a lack of involvement leading to their child's limited academic success. Sadly, this deficit perspective is widely used today as an explanation for the "achievement gap" (Valdes, 1996).

Families are involved in their children's learning at home. However, family involvement means different things to different people and families may be confused and have misunderstandings about their role in the school system (Valdes, 1996). For example, in many cultures, questioning the school or the teacher about curricular issues is considered disrespectful to the school authority (Han, 2007). This leads to an impasse of communication.

Unless the school system reaches out to communicate with families, many have very few ways of knowing school expectations or how to most appropriately support their children's academic growth (Ferguson, 2005). Indeed, when school systems establish ways to communicate with families, they have found parents extremely willing to spend more time on school-based learning activities with their children, especially if they are given some guidance from educators (Christensen, Hurley, Sheridan, & Fenstermacher, 1997). In the 1980s, Epstein (1986) stated that parents want to be more involved in their child's learning. Since then, research has consistently revealed that all families want to support their children's academic success, regardless of ethnicity, cultural background, or economic status (Ferguson, 2005).

EVERYDAY LEARNING SUPPORTS
CHILDREN'S SCHOOL SUCCESS

The way families prepare children for the transition to kindergarten is integral for ensuring success in a demanding new school environment (Ramey & Ramey, 1999). Simply engaging in one-on-one interactions with one's child can provide many opportunities for learning (Carnegie Task Force Meeting on the Needs of Young Children, 1994; Vukelich, Christie, & Enz, 2008). For early literacy, James Gee (2004) suggests:

Children who learn to read successfully do so because, for them learning to read is a cultural and not primarily an instructed process. Furthermore, this cultural process has long roots at home which have grown strong and firm before the child has walked in to a school. (p. 13)

Learning is a part of everyday family culture.

Daily routines and customs of the family are the first lessons children learn. Family routines and customs reflect a larger societal culture in which the family resides. Lev Vygotsky (1978) and Jean Piaget (1974) suggest that a child's culture teaches her/him what and how to think. Therefore, a child's culture directly affects cognitive development. As Walberg (1984) concluded, when families engage in problem-solving experiences in a "curriculum of the home" they promote high achievement in school.

Early literacy and numeracy "lessons" include parent–child conversations about everyday events and activities. Everyday activities can include setting the table, going to the library, reading a book, playing "I Spy" games in the car, measuring ingredients when making dinner, and pouring liquid in different-size plastic containers in the bathtub. All of these activities regularly take place at home, at no cost to families, and can create valuable learning opportunities for children. The conditions for meaningful learning improves even more when families are aware of the importance and value these simple activities have in helping their children become ready for school (Enz & Stamm, 2004). Any parent can plant the seeds of success.

EXAMPLES OF EARLY HOME LEARNING

What do these activities consist of? What do they look like? Let us consider two examples.

> **1:** "Ok, Tye, the recipe says add three cups of water. One, two, three! You can stir the mixture! Let's stir it 10 times. Let's count." (Mom says to 2-year-old daughter)
>
> **2:** "Dad, put this on your list and here's a coupon. I want to eat this for lunch" (says 4-year-old Aldo to dad). "Dad, your writing doesn't look like the coupon. Did you really write it?"

What are Tye and Aldo learning? Tye's mom is helping her to realize how print, in the form of recipes, help them make dinner and somehow counting, pouring, and stirring play a big role in this effort called dinner. Aldo has learned that going to the grocery store similarly involves lists and writing (on coupons); all are needed in order to get the food products he wants in the refrigerator.

These parents are supporting their children's learning by teaching important informal lessons. Families often stimulate learning through these basic everyday tasks. Research suggests that when families know the important role these tasks play in helping their children learn to read, write, understand math, etc., the more likely they are to consistently engage in these types of activities with their children at home (Enz, Mullady, & Rhodes, 2005). Ultimately, these early family learning experiences have more than a positive initial impact, but a lasting one on their children's academic careers (Enz et al., 2005; Henderson, & Berla, 1994; Lloyd, Steinberg, & Wilhelm-Chapin, 1999; Marcon, 1999). Given the importance of these learning experiences, families and children can benefit from programs that promote families' involvement in their children's learning at home. They may also need additional supports to enhance their children's development and overall well-being, increasing the likelihood of school success.

PROGRAMS TO PREPARE CHILDREN FOR SCHOOL SUCCESS

The transition to school is a process that families, teachers, and schools create and participate in, rather than an event that happens solely to the child (Pianta, Rimm-Kauffman, & Cox, 1999). Thoughtful, well-planned transition programs can help ensure success in school. Many programs have been developed over the past 40 years to help children and communities develop strong home-to-school transitions; programs where families, childcare providers, and schools all work together to ensure that the transition to school is smooth (Pianta et al., 1999; Neuman & Roskos, 1994; Ramey & Ramey, 1999).

Hundreds of programs have been developed at the national, state, and local levels in order to help children prepare for success in school. After reviewing more than 100 programs, using the research literature and a focused Web search, we broke these programs into three broadly categorized programs based on an analysis of their general features:

- *Family support programs* focus on the needs of the entire family, providing a range of services, including parent education, adult education, and family health care services.
- *Family interactive programs* focus on both parent and child working/playing together through an interactive curriculum.
- *Traditional parent education programs* provide school readiness information directly to parents.

Below, we provide illustrative examples of programs in each category. These exemplars, representative of programs at the national, state, and local levels, have as their primary mission a focus on helping families prepare young children (birth to age 5) for success in school. We describe each program and highlight the common features that lend to the success of the programs in each category.

FAMILY SUPPORT PROGRAMS

A number of comprehensive family support programs have been developed since the 1960s to serve low socioeconomic populations. These programs focus on the needs of the entire family and provide a range of services, including parent education, adult education, and family health care services. Often they target ethnic and/or language-minority families. The four programs highlighted below have been serving fairly large populations with exemplary results. These programs are AVANCE, EduCare, Schools of the 21st Century, and Supporting Partnerships to Assure Ready Kids (SPARK).

AVANCE

AVANCE is a Spanish word meaning "to advance" or "to progress." It is a nationally recognized nonprofit organization that was established in 1973. The AVANCE Parent–Child Education Program is considered a pioneer in the field of parent education. AVANCE reaches more than 20,000 individuals annually in sites throughout Texas and Los Angeles, California. AVANCE's 9-month-long parent education curriculum guides families through their children's stages of emotional, physical, social, and cognitive development, with special topics that cover school readiness, reading, effective discipline, and nutrition. The program serves predominantly lower socioeconomic Latino families. The program targets parents with children from birth to 3 years of age and operates in housing projects, community centers, and schools. Families are taught that they are the first and most important teachers for their children. They also attend courses that focus on the following topics: adult literacy, learning English as a second language, and obtaining a GED (AVANCE, 2006).

Thirty years of follow-up of program participants has provided strong evidence about the effectiveness of the AVANCE program. Results indicate that 100% of mothers who entered the program in 1973 (average fifth-grade education) went on to complete their GED and continued their education. Furthermore, the effects of AVANCE are generational: participants' children went on to excel in school; by 2001, 78% had either graduated from high school or earned a GED.

Educare

Beginning services to families in 2000, Educare is a relative newcomer. It combines funding sources from the federal government, Early Head Start, Head Start, state funding from local school districts, and private resources contributed by local philanthropies. This shared funding enables the community to provide exemplary early learning opportunities and better educational outcomes for children from birth to age 5. Educare has several sites, including Chicago, Omaha, Milwaukee, and Atlanta. Sites are staffed with educated professionals and operate with low staff-to-child ratios (1-to-3 for infants and toddlers and 1-to-6 for preschool-age children). Educare reaches out to parents, especially new mothers, teen mothers, and those receiving public assistance.

Early program evaluation focuses on children's academic growth, as well as families' learning. Findings indicate that Educare increases children's social and emotional skills and cognitive development, as well as improves parent–child relationships. Educare has increased parental involvement, family literacy activities, and the number of teen mothers completing high school. Also, it has improved parents' childrearing techniques. At the community level, Educare has reduced the need for remedial services and reduced public expenditures for abused and neglected children, as well as reduced juvenile delinquency (Educare, 2006).

Schools of the 21st Century

First launched in 1988, Schools of the 21st Century (21C), is one of the first national initiatives to blend the needs of families and support children's readiness for school. It was designed to respond to changes in patterns of work and family life in recent decades, especially the pressing need for working parents to have access to affordable, quality childcare. Since its inception, 21C has been implemented in more than 1,300 schools around the country, including urban, rural, and suburban areas. The overall goal of this multifaceted program is to promote the optimal growth and development of children beginning at birth. The flexibility of the 21C model enables individual schools to tailor the program to match their own needs and community resources. In many communities, 21C serves as an umbrella for an expanded array of family support services including adult education, youth development, and social services. The program features school-based preschool, before- and after-school care, family education, and social support services.

Initial and ongoing studies have found positive effects for family involvement, reduced parental stress, and positive academic outcomes for young children involved in the program (Schools of the 21st Century, 2002; Zigler, Finn-Stevenson, & Marsland, 1995). Children who participated in this program at age 3 were more likely to start kindergarten ready to learn (this was evidenced by their scores on kindergarten screening tests). Furthermore, children who participated in Schools of the 21st Century for at least 3 years obtained higher scores in mathematics and reading achievement tests than nonparticipating children.

Supporting Partnerships to Assure Ready Kids

Supporting Partnerships to Assure Ready Kids (The SPARK Program) is funded by the W.K. Kellogg Foundation and helps prepare children ages 3–5 for school. This program includes eight sites across the United States; each site serves at least 1,000 children. The main goal of the program is to ensure a smooth transition from home to school (SPARK, 2006). The program connects families with low incomes to early learning programs in schools and provides them with health and social services. SPARK also conducts developmental screenings and makes referrals to support in communication or language concerns, motor issues, and emotional/social problems (SPARK).

Overall, SPARK has been very successful in preparing children for school. Research conducted over the last few years has concluded that the program has successfully helped children be more prepared for the academic demands of school (SPARK, 2006). Families participating in the SPARK Program have been found to show an increase in the number of at-home learning activities and language opportunities they provided for their children. For example, over 61% of families that initially scored below the national median in learning materials used in the home now score at or above the median. Similarly, 80% of families that initially scored below the national median in language stimulation now score at, or above, the median; 100% of families initially scoring below the national median in academic stimulation now score at, or above, the median (SPARK, 2006).

Characteristics of Successful Family Support Programs

All the family support programs described above are resource intensive, requiring a significant initial financial commitment for the community.

However, their results strongly suggest that the initial financial investment is worthwhile. They lead to improved academic school success, as well as greatly reduce costs for health care, social, legal, and special education services.

After reviewing the above-mentioned programs, we determined that although family support programs vary in specific curriculum, they share common features that appear to be necessary for maximum program effectiveness. The following features are important for success:

- Quantity: the more of a program families can experience, the better.
- Duration: the longer the duration of a program and the greater the intensity, the better the program outcomes.
- Quality: includes high numbers of staff to provide enriching interactions with families and children.
- The earlier services begin, the better: the age of onset is very important, especially when considering children who may have special needs.
- Adult education: offered to families at the school, such as technology/vocational training, adult literacy and GED courses, and English as a second language/citizenship classes; provide additional opportunities for economic stability and employment options (Cooper, 1999).
- Transportation: many families living in low socio-economic communities do not have transportation, thus programs must either provide it or they must be located in close proximity to families' homes (Valdes, 1996).
- Free childcare and preschool programs: critical for allowing families to attend adult education programs (Cooper, 1999).

FAMILY INTERACTIVE PROGRAMS

Family interactive programs focus on the parent and child working/playing together through an interactive curriculum. Although it is a fairly new concept to include both families and children together in an interactive curriculum, these programs appear to stimulate more learning than traditional parent education programs because families are provided with hands-on materials to guide their parenting behaviors in the home. Likewise, these programs have found that when the children are involved in the workshops they tend to ask to repeat the activities at home. The family interactive programs we highlight here include Leaps and Bounds and the Even Start Family Literacy Program.

Leaps and Bounds

Leaps and Bounds was created in 2003 as a free, bilingual (Spanish-English) kindergarten readiness program in Phoenix, Arizona. It is offered to school and community sites serving families with low incomes and their children age 3–5. A small philanthropic grant through the Office of Youth Preparation at Arizona State University (ASU) supports the program. Currently, Leaps and Bounds has partnerships with over 40 different schools and social agencies in the Phoenix metropolitan area. Local school districts and college interns, who are earning field credit for admissions into ASU's teacher preparation program, provide instructional support. As of June 2008, the program has served over 435 families and their children.

The overarching goal of Leaps and Bounds is to ensure that children enter school ready to succeed by providing families with the information and support necessary to help them become their children's first teacher. Grounded in a constructivist approach, the program believes that families and children learn best when they interact together. The program strengthens the home–school relationship by promoting parental involvement in a family-centered environment. Participants engage in family-friendly activities that can be conducted in their homes at relatively no cost. The workshops are aligned with the Arizona Readiness and Kindergarten Standards in order to ensure that students have learned the knowledge included in these standards by the time they enter kindergarten. Although the workshops focus on the readiness skills of pre-kindergarteners, children between 3 and 5 years of age, the activities can be applied to children of various backgrounds and age groups.

Early results from the Leaps and Bounds program indicate that families are spending an increased amount of time facilitating similar learning experiences at home. The program has successfully increased the amount of family involvement at home by 1–3 hours each week. Families report spending an increased amount of time reading to their children, talking to their children, and engaging their children in school-like activities that promote language, social, and math skills. Furthermore, participants have commented that they feel "more important" and "empowered" to act as their children's first teacher (Enz et al., 2005). Interestingly, families have reported that their children appear to be the initiator of the everyday activities in their homes, often asking if they could do *"that counting thing again."* Moreover, families claim that they now feel comfortable learning with their children outside of school and in the home environment (Rhodes, Enz, & LaCount, 2006).

Even Start Family Literacy Program

Even Start is a federally funded family literacy program designed to br both the cycle of poverty and illiteracy by improving educational oppo nities for families and their children birth through age 7. The U.S. partment of Education funds the project. Families pay no fees. Even provides a broad range of services to the most-in-need families and t children. In 2007 there were approximately 1,300 Even Start programs tionwide, providing support services to over 50,000 families. Even Start fers an integrated program of adult literacy or adult basic education, ea childhood education, and parenting education. These components are i plemented through cooperative projects that build on existing commun resources to promote achievement of National Education Goals (Griswo & Ullman, 1997). To be eligible, at least one parent must participate in a three components of the Even Start project: early childhood activities, par enting, and adult education.

Research conducted over the past 5 years has demonstrated that for chil dren participating in this program, the achievement gap is narrowing— over 85% of the Even Start children read on grade level by the end of the primary grades (U.S. Department of Education, 1998).

Characteristics of Successful Family Interactive Programs

The family interactive programs discussed above aim to help children su ceed in school. While they vary in curriculum, they share common charac teristics that appear to be necessary for program effectiveness. Both reflect constructivist view of teaching and learning: families and children work wit program facilitators to solve problems and create new knowledge together, doing so in social environments that are sensitive to cultural customs and val ues, actively incorporating family input (Rhodes et al., 2006; Roskos & Neu man, 1993). These programs share the following features for success:

- Highly qualified family facilitators with training in program proce dures and goals.
- Opportunities to empower families in their role as first teacher.
- Curriculum that is responsive to the child's needs and emotions.
- Model activities that incorporate and validate learning materials found in the home.
- Activities that encourage positive parent– child interaction (co- construction).
- Activities that families and children can conduct at home.

TRADITIONAL PARENT EDUCATION PROGRAMS

Traditional parent education programs provide school readiness information directly to families. During parent education classes, families learn
new behaviors and skills that are central to creating long-term positive
changes in their parenting abilities. Parenting education is believed to
be an effective method to help families improve their parenting responsibilities and increase positive outcomes for children's long-term well-being
(Detroit Community Justice Partnership, 2005). The traditional parent
education programs we include here are the First Teacher Project and
Parent University.

First Teacher Project

Beginning in 1998, the First Teacher Project (FTP) provides parent education courses throughout the state of Arizona. It is supported through a
nonprofit organization, the New Directions Institute for Infant Brain Development (NDI). The project's premise is based on the belief that families
who understand *why* early stimulation is important and *how* to successfully
engage in activities with children will establish a secure bond with their children. In six sessions, typically ranging over 2 months, the program shares
information on early brain development with families of all socioeconomic
levels as well as childcare providers. Brain research is translated into com-
prehensible information that helps participants understand how children's
brains develop. The six 90-minute courses are shared with over 1,000 family members each year. The courses help support and nurture cognitive
growth by providing natural activities that focus a child's attention, increase
bonding, and improve language development through increased communication (Enz, 2003; Enz & Stamm, 2004; Stamm, 2007).

Research on the First Teacher Project reveals that families are spending
significantly more time in learning activities with their infants and toddlers.
Moreover, participating families are sharing the new information they received with family and friends (New Directions Institute for Infant Brain
Development, 2006).

Parent University

The purpose of Parent University, established in the late 1990s under
the management of the Detroit Community Justice Partnership program, is
to strengthen and improve parenting knowledge and skills. This program
focuses on the idea that parenting education is an effective method to help

families improve their parenting responsibilities and shape positive outcomes for their children's long-term well-being. Presented over 8 weeks, the Parent University curriculum includes child development, time management, stress management, effective communication strategies, social and emotional development, financial management, and health/nutrition.

Though a relatively new program, the results are positive. Families report improved relationships with their children. Also, they indicate a greater ability to communicate with their children and help their children improve their self-esteem. Furthermore, families note that their children are more able to resist negative peer pressure (Detroit Community Justice Partnership, 2005).

Characteristics of Successful Parent Education Programs

Virtually all states offer some form of parent education programs. Successful programs not only work to ensure families are provided with information necessary to be better parents, but they also work to ensure a child's success in school (Kumpher & Alvarado, 1998). Parent education programs often serve as bridges to other support programs that provide other educational opportunities to families. After reviewing the above parent educational programs, we found the following features useful for maximizing positive outcomes:

- Relating parenting skills to children's success in school.
- Providing families with activities that promote their children's learning.
- Including hands-on materials.
- Programs that are facilitator-led and highly interactive (not a lecture format).
- Having families share how they used materials at home (Enz et al., 2003).

COMMON THEMES GUIDING SUCCESSFUL FAMILY SUPPORT PROGRAMS

All three categories of programs—family support, family interactive, and traditional parent education—focus on the needs of the family. While some programs forefront socioemotional issues, or highlight health, safety, and nutrition issues, all address children's educational success in school settings. When comparing these programs, two promising practices emerge: the "system ready" concept and receptive systems.

System Ready Concept

All of these programs exhibit a "system ready" perspective. In other words, they don't simply expect children to be ready for school with academic skills, but instead these programs believe that the community has an obligation to serve children and their families in preparing for school (Swadener, 2006). The communities in which these programs are located are sensitive to the needs of families and have found multiple ways to provide support (Cooper, 1999; Schorr, 1998). Programs operating with a "system ready" perspective eliminate the belief that families are "lacking." Instead, they view families as partners in the process and focus on how the community can support the needs of its families (Gonzalez et al., 2005).

Receptive Systems

Receptive systems go beyond a readiness curriculum. In addition to offering family-friendly and welcoming environments, receptive systems hire professionals who are culturally competent (Cross, Bazron, Dennis, & Isaacs, 1989). Cultural competence requires professionals to demonstrate openness and flexibility regarding cultural differences, family structures, and languages (National Maternal and Child Health Center on Cultural Competency, 1997). Receptive systems and professionals go beyond providing a safe environment for families and offer proactive support for families. Receptive systems and professionals are alert to the needs of families and respond rapidly by becoming agents to connect families with needed social and medical services. Finally, receptive systems use the knowledge of the families they serve to build programs that respect and reflect the families' views of schooling; their values, beliefs, communication styles, childrearing and socialization practices, as well as their attitudes toward formal education (Ferguson, 2005).

CONCLUSION

Helping families to be successful in their role as their children's first teacher is critical to the social fabric of our communities. Schools, teachers, and communities are all responsible for helping children transition successfully from home to school (Pianta et al., 1999). Programs of all types and with a range of funding sources have been enacted in virtually every corner of the United States. All of these programs, to some degree, help families to prepare their children for success in kindergarten and beyond (Connell & Prinz, 2002; Henderson & Berla, 1994; Pianta et al., 1999; Ramey & Ramey, 1999; Snow, Burns, & Griffin, 1998). Families, teachers, schools, and communities must work together to ensure their children are ready for the transition from the home to school. Because a child's readiness for kindergarten depends in large part on the their support systems at home and in the community, programs that assist families with their efforts to provide their children with educational experiences are essential to our society's growth and success (Enz et al., 2003).

REFERENCES

Ackerman, D., & Barnett, W.S. (2005). *Prepared for kindergarten: What does "readiness" mean?* Head Start Information and Publication Center National Institute for Early Education Research (NIEER). Retrieved September 28, 2006, from http://nieer.org/resources/policyreports/report5.pdf

Avance. (2006). *What is Avance?* San Antonio, TX: Author. Retrieved August 15, 2006, from www.avance.org

Bloch, M. N. (1987). Becoming scientific and professional: An historical perspective on the aims and effects of early education. In T. S. Popkewitz (Ed.), *The formation of the school subjects* (pp. 25–62). London: Falmer Press.

Bracey, G. W. (2000). A children's garden no more. *Phi Delta Kappan, 81*(9), 712–713.

Byrant, D. M., & Clifford, R. M. (1992). 150 years of kindergarten: How far have we come? *Early Childhood Research Quarterly, 7*, 147–154.

Cannella, G. (2002). *Deconstructing early childhood education: social justice and revolution.* New York: Peter Lang.

Carnegie Task Force Meeting on the Needs of Young Children. (1994). *Starting points: Meeting the needs of our youngest children.* New York: Carnegie Corporation of New York.

Christensen, S., Hurley, C., Sheridan, S., & Fenstermacher, K. (1997). Parents and school psychologists' perspectives on parent involvement activities. *School Psychology Review, 26*, 111–130.

Coleman, J. (1966). *Equality of educational opportunity.* Washington, DC: Government Printing Office.

Connell, C., & Prinz, R. (2002). The impact of childcare and parent-child interactions on school readiness and social skills development for low-income African American children. *Journal of School Psychology, 40*(2), 177–193.

Cooper, C. (1999, Fall/Winter). Beyond the bake sale: How parent involvement makes a difference. *North Central Regional Educational Laboratory's Learning Point, 1*(3), 1–6.

Cross T., Bazron, B., Dennis, K., & Isaacs, M. (1989). *Towards a culturally competent system of care* (Vol. I). Washington, DC: Georgetown University Child Development Center, CASSP Technical Assistance Center.

Detroit Community Justice Partnership. (2005). *Parent University Evaluation Results.* Detroit, MI: Author. Retrieved May 17, 2006, from http://www.detroitcommunity justicepartnership.net

Diamond, K. E., Reagan, A. J., & Bandyk, J. E. (2000). Parents' conceptions of kindergarten readiness: Relationships with race, ethnicity, and development. *Journal of Educational Research, 94*(2), 8.

Educare (2006). *Educare.* Omaha, NE: Author. Retrieved December 14, 2006, from http://www.educareomaha.com/news.asp

Egertson, H. A. (1987). The shifting kindergarten curriculum. ERIC Digest. ERIC Clearinghouse on Elementary and Early Childhood Education [Online]. Retrieved December 27, 2006, from http://readyweb.crc.uiuc.edu/library/ pre1990/egertson.html

Elkind, D. (1986). Formal education and early childhood education: An essential difference. *Phi Delta Kappan. 67*(9), 631–636.

Enz, B. J. (2003). The A B C's of family literacy. In A. DeBruin-Pareki & B. Krol-Sinclair (Eds.), *Family literacy: From theory to practice* (pp. 32–51). Newark, DE: International Reading Association.

Enz, B.J., Mullady, A., & Rhodes, M. (2005, March). *Learning in leaps and bounds.* Paper presented at the annual meeting of the Association of Childhood Education International, Washington, DC.

Enz, B. J., Perry, N. J., & Yi, H. (2003). *Kindergarten readiness: A review of the literature and recommendations for educational outreach program designs.* Tempe: Arizona Board of Regents for Arizona State University and Office of Youth Preparation.

Enz, B. J., & Stamm, J. (2004, May). *Supporting parents as first literacy teachers: From cradle to kindergarten.* Paper presented at the annual meeting of the International Reading Association, Reno, NV.

Epstein, J. L. (1986). Parents' reactions to teacher practices of parent involvement. *The Elementary School Journal, 86,* 277–294.

Ferguson, C. (2005). *Reaching out to diverse populations: What can schools do to foster family-school connections?* A Strategy Brief of the National Center for Family and Community Connections with Schools. SEDL. Austin, TX. Retrieved January 21, 2007, from http://www.sedl.org/connections

Gee, J. (2004). *Situated language and learning.* New York: Routledge.

Gonzalez, N., Moll, L., Tenery, M., Rivera, A., Rendon, P., Gonzales, R., et al. (2005). Funds of knowledge for teaching in Latino households. In N. Gonzalez, L. Moll, & C. Amanti (Eds.), *Funds of knowledge: Theorizing practices in households, communities, and classrooms* (pp. 89–118). Hillsdale, NJ: Erlbaum.

Griswold, K., & Ullman, C. M. (1997). *Not a one-way street: The power of reciprocity in family literacy programs.* New York: Bronx City University of New York. (ERIC Document Reproduction Service No. ED413420)

Han, M. (2007). Promoting parent involvement in culturally and linguistically diverse classrooms: Birth–kindergarten. In C. Vukelich, J. Christie, & B. Enz (Eds.), *Helping young children learn language and literacy* (pp. 237–240). Boston: Allyn & Bacon.

Henderson, A. T., & Berla, N. (1994). *A new generation of evidence: The family is critical to student achievement.* Washington, DC: National Committee for Citizens in Education. (ERIC Document Reproduction Service No. ED375968).

Katz, L., Raths, J. D., & Torres, R. T. (1987). *A place called kindergarten.* Urbana, IL: ERIC Clearinghouse on Elementary and Early Childhood Education. (ERIC Document Reproduction No. ED280595)

Kumpfer, K. L., & Alvarado, R. (1998). *Effective family strengthening interventions.* OJJ-DP Juvenile Justice Bulletin [NCJ 171121]. Washington, DC: U.S. Department of Justice, Office of Justice Programs, Office of Juvenile Justice and Delinquency Prevention.

Lloyd, J. W., Steinberg, D., & Wilhelm-Chapin, M. K. (1999). Research on transition to kindergarten. In R. C. Pianta & M. Cox (Eds.), *The transition to kindergarten* (pp.305–316). Baltimore: Paul H. Brookes.

Logsdon, J. (1998, Spring). Parent involvement…so much more than ever before. *Research Center for Families and Children Spring Newsletter. Families and Children.* College of Human Environmental Sciences, Lexington, KY.

Marcon, R. (1998, July). *Predicting parent involvement and its influence on school success: A follow-up study.* Poster presented at the Fourth National Head Start Research Conference, Washington, DC.

Marcon, R. A. (1999). Positive relationships between parent school involvement and public school inner-city preschoolers' development and academic performance. *School Psychology Review, 28*(3), 395–412.

Moyer, J. (1999). *The child-centered kindergarten.* ACEI position paper. Association for Childhood Education International, Retrieved July 29, 2006, from www.acei.org/cckind.htm

NAEYC. (1995). *School readiness.* Washington, DC: National Association for the Education of Young Children. Retrieved July 30, 2006, from www.naeyc.org/about/positions/pdf/Psunacc.pdf

National Center for Early Development and Learning. (1998). *Multi-state study of pre-kindergarteners.* Chapel Hill, NC. Retrieved October 30, 2006, from http://www.fpg.unc.edu/~ncedl

National Education Panel. (1995). *National Education Goals Panel.* North Central Regional Educational Laboratory (NCREL). Retrieved October 10, 2006, from http://www.ncrel.org/sdrs/areas/issues/envrnmnt/go/go4negp.htm

National Maternal and Child Health Center on Cultural Competency. (1997). *North Carolina Division of Child Development data.* Raleigh: North Carolina Division of Child Development. Retrieved June 27, 2006, from http://ncchildcare.dhhs.state.nc.us/general/home.asp

National Maternal and Child Health Resource Center on Cultural Competency. (1997). *Journey towards cultural competency: Lessons learned.* Vienna, VA: Maternal and Children's Health Bureau Clearinghouse.

Neuman, S. B., & Roskos, K. (1994). Bridging home and school with a culturally responsive approach. *Childhood Education, 70*(4), 210–214.

New Directions Institute for Infant Brain Development. (2006). *New Directions Institute for Infant Brain Development.* Scottsdale, AZ: Author. Retrieved October, 17, 2006, from www.newdirectionsinstitute.org

Oden, S., Schweinhart, L., & Weikart, D. (2000). *Into adulthood: A study of the effects of Head Start.* Ypsilanti, MI: High/Scope Educational Research.

Olmsted, P. P. (1991). Parent involvement in elementary education: Findings and suggestions from the Follow Through Program. *Elementary School Journal, 9*(3), 221–231.

Piaget, J. (2000). The place of the sciences commentary on Vygotsky. *New Ideas in Psychology, 18*(2-3), 241–259.

Pianta, R. C., &. Cox, M. J. (1999). The changing nature of the transition to school: Trends for the next decade. In R. C. Pianta & M. J. Cox (Eds.), *The transition to kindergarten* (pp. 363-79). Baltimore: Paul H. Brookes.

Pianta, R. C., Rimm-Kauffman, S. E., & Cox, M. J. (1999). Introduction: An ecological approach to kindergarten transition. In R. C. Pianta & M. J. Cox (Eds.), *The transition to kindergarten* (pp. 3–12). Baltimore: Paul H. Brookes.

Piotrokowski, C. S., Botsko, M., & Matthews, E. (2001). Parents' and teachers' beliefs about children's school readiness in a high-need community. *Early Childhood Research Quarterly, 15*(4), 537–558.

Ramey, C. T., & Ramey, S. L. (1999). Beginning school for children at risk. In R. C. Pianta & M. J. Cox (Eds.), *The transition to kindergarten* (pp. 217–251). Baltimore: Paul H. Brookes.

Rhodes, M., Enz, B. J. & LaCount, M. (2006). Leaps and Bounds: Preparing parents for kindergarten. *Young Children 61*(1), 50–51.

Roskos, K., & Neuman, S. (1993). Descriptive observations of adults' facilitation of literacy in play. *Early Childhood Research Quarterly, 8,* 77–97.

Schorr, E. (1998). *Common purpose: Strengthening families and neighborhoods to rebuild America.* New York: Anchor Books.

Schools of the 21st Century. (2002). *Research on the efficacy of Schools of the 21st Century.* New Haven, CT. Retrieved March 10, 2006, from http://www.yale.edu/bushcenter/21C/history.html

Schweinhart, L. J., Montie, J., Xiang, Z., Barnett, W. S., Belfield, C. R., & Nores, M. (2005). *Lifetime effects: The High Scope Perry Preschool study through age 40.* Ypsilanti, MI: High/Scope Press.

Seitz, V., Rosenbaum, L. K., & Apfel, N. H. (1985). Effects of family support intervention: A ten-year follow-up. *Child Development, 56*(2), 376–391.

Snow, C., Burns, S., & Griffin, P. (1998). *Preventing reading difficulties in young children.* Washington, DC: National Academic Press.

SPARK. (2006). *SPARK: Supporting Partnerships to Assure Ready Kids.* Battle Creek, MI: W.K. Kellogg Foundation. http://www.wkkf.org/default.aspx?tabid=71&CID=168&NID=54&LanguageID=0

Stamm, J. (2007). *Bright from the start, the simple science-backed way to nurture your child's developing mind from birth to age three.* New York: Gotham Press.

Swadener, E.B. (2006). "Keeping it real" in early childhood professional development: Lessons from the Arizona System Ready/Child Ready Project: Contexts for AzSRCR: Challenges and opportunities in Arizona. Paper presented at the annual meeting of the American Educational Research Association, San Francisco.

U.S. Department of Education. (1998). *National evaluation of the Even Start Family Literacy Program.* Retrieved October 11, 2006, from http://www.ed.gov/pubs/evenstart_final/exc.html.

Valdes, G. (1996). *Con respeto: Bridging the distances between culturally diverse families and schools: An ethnographic portrait.* New York: Teachers College Press.

Vukelich, C., Christie, J., & Enz, B. (2008). *Helping young children learn language and literacy.* Boston: Allyn & Bacon.

Vygotsky, L. (1978). *Mind in society: The development of psychological processes.* Cambridge, MA: Harvard University Press.

Walberg, H. J. (1984). Families as partners in educational productivity. *Phi Delta Kappan, 65*(6), 397–400.

Zigler, E. F., Finn-Stevenson, M., & Marsland, K.W. (1995). Child day care. *Journal of Children and Poverty 1*(1), 29–60.

TESCO
extra

SWINDON

===================

SALES VOUCHER
CUSTOMER COPY

===================

```
CARD TYPE : VISADEBIT
AID       : A0000000031010
NUMBER    : *************7876      ICC
PAN SEQ NO : 00
AUTH CODE : 088254
MERCHANT  : 46323042
START : 03/13  EXPIRY : 03/16
Cardholder PIN Verified
```

GOODS: £32.00

TOTAL: £32.00

How did we do?
Visit www.tescocomments.com and
tell us about your shopping trip

24/01/14 15:30 3230 118 7006 6557

www.tesco.com

VAT NO: 220430231

THANK YOU FOR SHOPPING
WITH US

Mixed Sources
Product group from well-managed
forests and other controlled sources
www.fsc.org Cert no.SGS-COC-005999
© 1996 Forest Stewardship Council

TESCO

Every little helps

If you change your mind about
your purchase, please retain
your receipt and return it to the
store with the product as sold
within 28 days.
Conditions apply to some products,
please see Instore for details.
Your statutory rights are not
affected.

Tesco Stores Ltd
Registered Office
Tesco House, Delamare Road
Cheshunt, Herts. EN8 9SL
www.tesco.com

VAT NO: 220430231

THANK YOU FOR SHOPPING
WITH US

Mixed Sources

CHAPTER 5

HOME-BASED CARE PLAYS AN IMPORTANT ROLE IN MEETING FAMILY NEEDS

Lori Connors-Tadros and Dawn Ramsburg[1]

INTRODUCTION

Research indicates that parental characteristics (i.e., parent education, parental nurturance and warmth) have a greater influence on children's development than any particular child care setting (National Institute of Child Health and Human Development Early Child Care Research Network, 2007). However, as increasing numbers of mothers have entered the workforce and placed their children in nonparental care, researchers and policymakers have begun to address the role of caregivers in supporting child development and strengthening family involvement in early care and education. Home-based care is the predominant child care choice for parents of infants and toddlers, particularly for low-income and minority families (Brandon, 2005).

Research on home-based care as a distinct form of child care is primarily descriptive (i.e., demographics about parents and providers) and the experimental literature is sparse, particularly with reference to the impact on family involvement practices. Child care research historically has viewed

Promising Practices for Partnering with Families in the Early Years, pages 79–102
Copyright © 2008 by Information Age Publishing
All rights of reproduction in any form reserved.
79

family involvement from a program (i.e., center-based) perspective focusing on factors that support overall quality of care, including family involvement practices such as attendance at center-based meetings or parent conferences. Home-based child care, however, draws more heavily on principles of family support from family systems theory and ecological theories of development, which posit that families are children's most important teachers and are equal partners in the caregiving relationship. Family-centered practice recognizes that families' unique values and needs are strengths upon which to build relationships and improve family functioning and child well-being. Families are more likely to be actively involved with program services when they feel valued and treated as if they are knowledgeable and capable (Green, McAllister, & Tarte, 2004). Yet, because home-based care is often provided by an extended family member, such traditional approaches to improving family involvement in early childhood settings as participation on parent advisory boards are not applicable.

Home-based care offers unique opportunities for family and community involvement, but these have yet to be given adequate attention in research or practice. This chapter provides information on the distinctions across home-based care. Key policy mechanisms to improve the quality of home-based care are discussed in light of the opportunities for impacting family and community involvement practices. The final section of the chapter identifies statewide systemic approaches, inclusive of all practitioners, and community-based, targeted models, that integrate goals related to family and community involvement in efforts to improve quality in home-based care settings. The chapter concludes with a discussion of the implications for practice and future research directions.

HISTORICAL PERSPECTIVE AND CURRENT REALITY

Home-based care is the oldest form of child care and reflects the dual role child care plays for many American families—a service to parents that enables them to go to work and a service to children that impacts their development and general well-being. Parents who use home-based care are seeking to maintain an environment that resembles the family environment while they are away from their children (Mensing, French, Fuller, & Kagan, 2000). They also want to be sure their children are safe, well cared for, growing, and learning. Some home-based caregivers are paid to work with small groups of children in their homes as businesses contributing to the local economy, and these include grandparents, aunts, and others who open their homes daily to help family members. These services are often offered for free or in exchange for other services (Annie E. Casey Foundation, 2006).

Care in the home offers families some distinct advantages, depending on family needs (e.g., number of children in family), parent needs (e.g., work hours), and parent preferences (e.g., trust of provider). Children in home-based care experience relatively stable care arrangements. A recent study of child care for families with low incomes found that half of the children cared for by relatives had been in a single care arrangement since birth (Layzer & Goodson, 2006). As with other settings, there are policy concerns about home-based care, ranging from the educational opportunities available to children to the level of training required of the caregiver. Programs that oversee child care regulations and administer family assistance programs work to balance resources to provide families access to a wide range of child care settings while ensuring the settings promote positive children's development.

What Is Home-Based Care?

In addition to basic facility distinctions (care occurs in a home residence), home-based care also is distinguished from center care by the number of children in care and the relationship between the children and provider. Whereas child care centers have multiple classrooms and a variety of staff—director, teachers, and support staff such as janitors and cooks—home-based care involves a home setting (house or apartment) where a small number of children are cared for, and often includes the provider's own children or other related children (Layzer & Goodson, 2006). State definitions for home-based care vary tremendously based on the location of care (i.e., in the child's home or the caregiver's home), the relationship between the child and provider (i.e., relative or nonrelative), and thresholds for regulation (i.e., number of children or families in care or the number of hours of care to be exempt from regulation).

Consequently, the term *home-based care* encompasses all of the following arrangements, which are not mutually exclusive, as demonstrated in Figure 5.1:

- In-home care—Care occurs in the child's home; it may be provided by a relative or nonrelative, including *au pairs* and nannies.[2]
- Family, friend, and neighbor (FFN) care, including the following:
- Relative care ("kin")—Care occurs in either the child's home or in the relative's home.
- Care by friends and neighbors ("kith")—Care occurs in the child's home or in the friend or neighbor's home.
- Family child care (FCC; also called family day care)—Care in the provider's home for unrelated children (may also include FCC group homes); typically the only home-based care regulated by states.

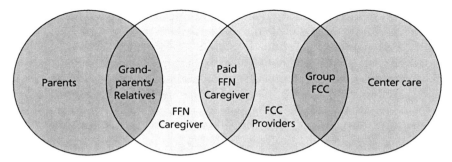

Figure 5.1 Continuum of child care. *Source:* Adapted from T. Porter & R. Rice (2000). *Lessons learned: Strategies for working with kith and kin caregivers.* New York, NY: Bank Street College of Education.

In this chapter, the term *home-based care* is used to include all forms of care occurring in a home, whether by a relative or nonrelative and whether regulated or not regulated. When additional details are known about the characteristics of the home-based care arrangement, one of the more specific terms above is used.

What is the Prevalence of Home-Based Care?

Variation in terminology for home-based care complicates the national picture of the number and characteristics of home-based arrangements and caregivers. Several national datasets estimate home-based care use, but each collapses home-based care categories differently. State datasets typically track only those home-based settings that are regulated and/or paid, excluding thousands of unregulated and unpaid relative and in-home settings. Furthermore, many datasets fail to adequately distinguish facility data from individual caregiver data so information on the number and characteristics of the home-based caregivers is quite sparse.[3]

Examining all children under age 5 in the United States, almost two out of every three children are in some form of nonparental care arrangement on a regular basis (Johnson, 2005). Among those, home-based care is used by approximately half the families regardless of family income (Iruka & Carver, 2006; Johnson, 2005), with about one-third using relative caregivers. Looking at families receiving financial assistance to pay for child care, approximately two out of five families use home-based care, with more than half (56%) of those children in unregulated home-based settings cared for by relatives (Child Care Bureau, 2005).

The Human Services Policy Center and the Center for the Child Care Workforce estimated there were approximately 2.5 million caregivers in

2001, with three-fourths in home-based settings (Center for the Child Care Workforce & Human Services Policy Center, 2002). To date, no nationally representative study of home-based caregivers has been conducted. In the few studies that exist looking solely at family child care providers, it is estimated that less than one-third have some formal college education and fewer than 15% have a bachelor's or associate's degree (Brandon & Martinez-Beck, 2005). Many states do not require home-based caregivers to meet any formal education or training requirements.[4]

Who Uses Home-Based Care?

Research finds several key family and child characteristics linked to the use of home-based care. Family size, hours worked, family income, family preferences, location, and age of children are all related to home-based care use. Families with more than one child more frequently use home-based care because of the convenience of having one location for picking-up and dropping-off their children, and so that siblings can stay together because of the mixed-age grouping allowed in homes.

Parents working nontraditional hours (during evenings, on weekends, and with rotating schedules from week to week) more frequently use home-based care because of the flexible hours of operation offered by home-based caregivers. Because parents with low incomes, including those transitioning from welfare to work, frequently work nontraditional hours, there is a link between family income and use of home-based care, with low-income parents more likely to use home-based care. Also, parents working these schedules report a preference for the family setting that home-based care offers because mealtime, bathtime, and bedtime rituals can be more easily accommodated.

Families living in rural areas are more likely to use home-based care as few rural settings can sustain a supply of centers given the smaller density of children in these areas (Atkinson, 1994; Smith, 2006). Finally, families with very young children (i.e., infants and toddlers) and families with school-age children are more likely to use home-based care. For younger children, home-based care may offer more personalized and individual attention since there are fewer children in the setting. For school-age children, home-based care offers a less structured environment before and after school, similar to the care they receive in their own homes.

Why Do Families Select Home-Based Care?

Such utilization patterns do not reveal the underlying reasons for why families choose home-based care. Choosing a child care arrangement is a personal decision involving family values about work, childrearing, and education, and is practically intertwined with considerations of work schedules, cost, and convenience. Parents weigh a complex set of factors including parental values (e.g., beliefs about childrearing), supply of available care (e.g., the range of child care options available in the community), parental preferences (e.g., child care close to work or home), constraints and barriers (e.g., cost and hours needed), and satisfaction with care once an arrangement is selected.

In an effort to more clearly understand families' decisions to use home-based care, some researchers have asked parents about their child care selection process. Many parents report they did not consider any other options when selecting their home-based care arrangement: 48% of parents using all types of home-based care in the *National Study of Child Care for Low-Income Families: Care in the Home* (Layzer & Goodson, 2006) and 70% of parents using family, friend, and neighbor care surveyed in Illinois (Anderson, Ramsburg, & Scott, 2005). Families using home-based care report that they knew their provider before the care arrangement began or that they learned about their provider from friends, relatives, neighbors, or another provider (Layzer & Goodson, 2006).

Numerous research surveys have included questions for parents about why they chose a particular arrangement (e.g., Anderson et al., 2005; Brandon, Maher, Joesch, & Doyle, 2002; Layzer & Goodson, 2006; Maxwell, 2005) to try to understand some of the advantages home-based care offers some families, although the underlying decision-making process of parental choice of child care is still not understood completely. It is this level of understanding that is important for determining implications and expectations for family involvement.

Home-based care often involves an ongoing relationship between the caregiver, parent and children that may not be found in center-based settings. When relatives and close friends provide care, there is a personal relationship beyond the child–caregiver relationship since the provider is sometimes part of family gatherings and rituals (e.g., birthday parties) outside the caregiving arrangement. In addition, parents who use regulated family child care report the support they receive from the caregiver as a positive benefit of the arrangement (e.g., having dinner sent home with the parent who had to work late when they pick up the children). Parents who select home-based care mention the shared culture, language, and values with their home-based caregivers as key reasons for their child care choice. Parents' racial and ethnic demographics frequently mirror provider demographics, suggesting families select caregivers similar to themselves.

Parents commonly cite safety as a key factor in their choice of care. Families selecting home-based care believe safety is ensured because they know and trust the provider (Butler, Bringham, & Schultheiss, 1991; Galinsky et al., 1994; Hofferth, Brayfield, Deitch, & Holcomb, 1991; Mensing, French, Fuller, & Kagan, 2000). Parents also report seeking caregivers they are comfortable with, who they believe will care for the child in a manner similar to their own, or who shares similar values and beliefs with them (Coley, Chase-Lansdale, & Li-Grinning, 2001; Galinsky et al., 1994; Hertz & Ferguson, 1996; Layzer & Goodson, 2006). Thus, efforts to support family involvement must acknowledge that in home-based settings, and particularly those with relative caregivers, multiple relationship dynamics (child–parent, child–caregiver, and parent–caregiver) need to be understood and supported.

FEDERAL AND STATE POLICY EFFORTS TO IMPROVE QUALITY

The field of early care and education as a coordinated system of supports to families and children has gained increased attention across the United States due to a number of economic, political, and social factors. As the number of mothers of young children entering the workforce has increased, the demand for child care has grown exponentially. In order to meet the demand for child care and support working families, policy has focused on efforts to ensure parents at all economic levels have a choice of care and education settings to meet their children's needs. Furthermore, brain research has elucidated the importance of certain characteristics of the environment and adult–child interactions that best support children's healthy development and learning. The United States is investing significant resources, at the local, state, and national levels, through public and private dollars, to increase access to high quality early care and education settings for all children (Adams, Tout, & Maslow, 2007).

Federal Policy Efforts

At the federal level, a number of programs address the early learning and care of young children. Head Start and Early Head Start provides comprehensive education services to children from families with low incomes, in a variety of settings, determined at the local level. The Child Care and Development Fund (CCDF),[5] authorized by the Child Care and Development Block Grant Act, and Section 418 of the Social Security Act, assists families with low-income, families receiving temporary public assistance, and those transitioning from public assistance in obtaining child care so parents can work or attend training/education. A fundamental principal of CCDF is ensuring parents have access to a choice of care settings to meet their child care needs. The Individuals with Disabilities Education Act (IDEA) provides infants and toddlers with disabilities (birth to age 2) and their families with early intervention services under IDEA Part C. Children and youth (ages 3–21) receive special education and related services under IDEA Part B. Services for children are determined at the local level to ensure children are placed in the "least restrictive environment" and for young children this often means center-based or family child care. Recent efforts at the federal level are moving toward greater coordination of the variety of early care and education funding streams and programs to ensure all children and their families have access to high-quality early learning environments in the settings that best serve their needs.

State-Level Policy Efforts

Child care policies related to home-based care are implemented at the state level through regulations related to licensing to ensure safety and basic healthy development, and at the federal level through rules and standards related to supporting families with low income and ensuring parental choice of the full range of child care settings. There is wide variation at the state level in both the range of authority over specific home-based care settings and the overall stringency of child care regulations and in the amount of funding and support for improving quality in all care settings (Edie, 2006). However, given recent research on the importance of early learning, the number of families using out-of-home care, and overall concerns with quality of care in all settings, there is a greater urgency in the policy arena to address these issues through targeted funding, policy priorities, technical assistance, and research. Examples of these efforts are discussed below.

Child Care Regulations

Each state is responsible for defining which home-based providers are subject to regulations, and then establishing those regulations for regulated family child care settings. Regulation, including licensing, certification, or registration of providers, typically addresses one or more of the following: child health and safety (e.g., child immunization, amount of space in caregiving environment, criminal background checks of provider), group size, ratios of children to adults, minimum age of caregiver, and minimum and ongoing training and education requirements for caregivers. Family communication and caregiver–parent interactions are typically included in state caregiver training requirements. For example, if a state requires regulated family child care providers to obtain a Child Development Associate (CDA) credential as a minimum training requirement, one of the competency standards of the CDA is "to establish positive and productive relationships with families."[6]

All 50 states exempt care by relatives from licensing requirements (Porter & Kearns, 2005). State thresholds for regulation of nonrelative family child care providers vary along three dimensions: the number of children in care at one time, the number of families, and the amount of time spent with the caregiver (Porter & Kearns, 2005).[7] In addition, many states impose health and safety requirements, outside of the licensing system, on home-based care providers caring for children receiving subsidies, including relative caregivers. For example, all home-based providers may be required to attend mandatory training or orientation sessions, even if they are not subject to licensing regulations, as a way to ensure minimum health and safety standards are met for children cared for in these settings.

Improving Quality

States have taken a variety of approaches to improve the quality of home-based care to support positive child development outcomes. Child care quality is driven by a number of factors; *caregiver characteristics* such as motivation for providing care and level of education and training; *process* elements caregiving such as caregiver–child interactions and caregiver–family interactions; and *structural* elements such as group size and child:adult ratio. These quality components have been investigated to understand their links to child outcomes as policymakers strive to ensure that children's early childhood experiences in all settings are supportive of school readiness. A key concern to researchers and policymakers is whether current quality measures and definitions adequately capture the distinctive elements of home-based care. For example, global measures of quality may not adequately capture certain characteristics of home-based settings, such as the role of mixed-age groupings of children or the degree of importance of shared beliefs about childrearing between family and caregivers. Consequently, policymakers must weigh many decisions about what elements of quality are important when they embark on quality improvement strategies.

At the federal level, the primary funding stream allocating resources to improve the quality of care is the Child Care and Development Fund (CCDF). Federal regulations require states to allocate "not less than 4%" of the state's block grant[8] to initiatives to improve quality in all care settings. States invested $920 million in FY 2005 (10% of total expenditures) in activities to assist providers to access professional development, comply with licensing regulations, and other activities to support quality (Child Care Bureau, 2006). Professional development, including initiatives and activities for individual practitioners and programs, as well as various efforts to strengthen the professional development and training system, are a major focus of states' investments in quality. Initiatives are focused both on providing training and professional development to increase emotionally supportive and responsive caregiving, as well as early learning. Overall, 97% of states had at least one initiative targeted to families, most often consumer education provided by child care resource and referral agencies to help families understand and choose quality care. Most of the states' quality activities are focused on center-based or regulated family child care providers (American Public Human Services Association & Child Trends, 2006).

APPROACHES TO IMPROVING QUALITY: OPPORTUNITIES FOR PARTNERING WITH FAMILIES

In response to federal and state policy initiatives, states and communities have undertaken a variety of efforts to improve the overall quality of early care and education, including home-based care. States attempt to align various elements of high-quality early care and education to meet the needs of children and families. Research has identified important systemic elements and approaches to a high-quality early care and education system, such as coordination among programs and funding streams, comprehensive professional development, quality rating systems, guidelines for children's learning, and models that target the specific needs of certain children and/or settings. These efforts often embed activities related to family and community involvement within the broader approach, rather than place a singular emphasis on family involvement. Nevertheless, the implications for practice are important for realizing goals for children and families and to provide direction for future research. In the following section, approaches and models to improving quality that appear to offer the greatest opportunity for strengthening family and community involvement are identified. This section identifies statewide systemic initiatives designed to be inclusive of all practitioners as well as community-based approaches that target specific types of practitioners and/or settings.

Statewide Systemic Initiatives—Inclusive of All Practitioners

Coordination of Funding and Programs

Multiple federal and state programs and funding streams within various government agencies fund early care and education services for young children. In the mid-to-late 1990s, states began to invest in strengthening the coordination within the early care and education system—to be inclusive of all settings where children spent time before entering public schools. Increasingly, private foundations (e.g., Annie E. Casey Foundation, Gates Foundation) have funded, individually or jointly with state funding, early care and education initiatives. These efforts are addressing the coordination of state agency infrastructures and public and private funding sources to improve quality and early learning opportunities in all care settings. Comprehensive services to support families and encourage family involvement are often included in the goals of these initiatives, reflecting family support/family-centered care principles. For example, North Carolina launched Smart Start in 1993 to support the health and school readiness of young children and to provide family support to parents. Funding is provided through state funding and private donations and administered by local nonprofit agencies. Local partnerships with representatives of the community and parents determine the specific design and delivery of early care and education services. Smart Start local partnerships implement a variety of efforts to support families by providing information on children's development, encouraging involvement of families in program design, and in providing training to practitioners on effective parent–provider relationships (Mitchell, 2005b). Other states have adapted the Smart Start model or developed similar approaches to providing comprehensive services to young children before they enter formal schooling.

Child Care Resource and Referral

Child care resource and referral (CCR&R) agencies play a role in supporting both families and child care providers. For over 20 years, child care resource and referral agencies have been established in communities across the United States to support families seeking child care (e.g., referrals to child care providers, information on child care quality, and information on financial assistance to pay for child care); to support child care providers (e.g., training, technical assistance, and financial assistance to child care providers to support quality improvement activities); to compile, analyze, and share child care information with parents, providers, and communities (e.g., maintain database of child care provider supply parents' child care needs and track trends); and to build partnerships in states to address its child care needs (e.g., collaborate with other family support services such as health, special needs to improve services for families). Initially, CCR&R agencies were created by employers to meet the child care needs of its workforce. Since 1996, CCDF has included targeted funds to support child care resource and referral agencies, including administering the CCDF program in some states and communities. As of 2006, there are 850 CCR&R agencies across the country and in every state; 38 states have statewide CCR&R networks; and 8 states have one or two CCR&Rs serving the entire state (National Association of Child Care Resource & Referral Agencies, 2006b). These CCR&Rs, which are designed to be responsive to the local child care needs of communities, combine their public (federal, state, or local) and private funds into a package of services for parents and providers that varies from community to community.

Standards for Early Learning

As a result of a presidential initiative in 2002, states and territories began to develop and/or revise early learning guidelines[9] to be "applicable to all care settings" including home-based settings. According to the most recent figures, 50 states, the District of Columbia, and 3 territories have developed early learning guidelines *applicable to all care settings* and 37 states and 1 territory are implementing their guidelines through dissemination or training or are embedding early learning guidelines in their professional development systems (Child Care Bureau, 2006).

Some states have developed innovative approaches to reach home-based practitioners with training on how to use early learning guidelines effectively to support children's development and to inform families of the role of standards in improving outcomes for children. For example, Rhode Island has developed a five-session series on using early learning guidelines to support children's development and family involvement, in English and Spanish, for family child care providers. In Minnesota, a public–private partnership to promote school readiness has focused on aligning early learning guidelines with training for home-based providers, including family, friend, and neighbor care providers. Most states have also developed materials for families, often in multiple languages and formats, to facilitate families' understanding and to encourage parents' use of early learning guidelines to guide their activities with their children at home and to increase parents' understanding of children's learning and development. In Maine, family child care providers developed a self-assessment tool aligned with the early learning standards to examine their own practice to support children in addressing the early learning standards. The tool is also used to observe children's progress and to communicate with families.

Comprehensive Professional Development Systems

More than 30 states are engaged in efforts to develop comprehensive professional development systems that include all early care and education practitioners, including regulated family child care and center-based care (i.e., Head Start, community-based care, state-funded prekindergarten). Cross-sector professional development systems align training, credentialing, and certification efforts targeted to the range of roles and responsibilities in all early care and education settings, and seek to increase access by all practitioners (Mitchell & LeMoine, 2005). Comprehensive professional development systems put in place the systemic supports for all practitioners to access the content knowledge and practical applications of key skills related to children's learning and family involvement.

The intent and expectations of these efforts is to provide a career pathway for all early care and education practitioners, allowing individuals to enter the system from a variety of points, and progress through the system acquiring increasing skills and competencies to provide a high-quality experience for children. Challenges that states are addressing in ensuring that home-based practitioners have access to the system include basic issues—such as costs, transportation, and child care—as well as addressing beliefs related to professional roles and higher education. Furthermore, in recognition of the unique qualities of home-based care environments and relationship with families, states are beginning to look to principles of family support and/or family and community involvement to design new strategies and approaches for supporting the continued education of home-based practitioners. In Delaware, Family Child Care Support Groups, coordinated by the state licensing office and led by an experienced family child care provider, addresses the need for information and support provided by peers.

Quality Rating Systems

A quality rating system (QRS) is a systemic approach to assess, improve, and communicate the level of quality in early care and education programs (National Child Care Information Center, 2007). QRSs offer state policymakers a strategic framework to align initiatives focused on quality improvement for all child care settings. A common goal of a QRS is to increase families' understanding of factors related to high quality care and most state and local systems include parent education and/or family involvement as an indicator of high quality. QRSs present an opportunity to strengthen relationships between families and care providers, in both supporting children's development and in improving the quality of care. The number of states currently implementing QRSs has grown to more than 14 and more than 25 states are actively discussing, developing, and/or piloting a QRS. Thirteen of the 14 statewide QRSs include regulated family child care homes in their rating systems.

Five elements are most often included in a QRS: (1) standards, (2) accountability, (3) program and practitioner outreach and support, (4) financing incentives linked to compliance with quality standards, and (5) parent education regarding the design of the Quality Rating system and how it benefits children and families (Mitchell, 2005a). In a review of state QRSs, the following criteria are most often used to indicate parent/family involvement: the availability of parent advisory boards, parent bulletin boards or newsletters, parent conferences and meetings, parent handbooks/written program policies, parent resource centers, parent satisfaction surveys, family-centered policies, and/or ways of sharing children's daily activities with parents (National Child Care Information Center, 2005).

Tennessee's Report Card Evaluation and Star Quality Child Care Program is a QRS that is mandatory for all regulated family child care homes, and has a specific goal related to family involvement. Mandated by law in 1991, the goals of the program are to encourage and recognize quality child care programs, improve child care quality statewide, and provide information to parents as they seek quality child care for their children. Family child care homes are evaluated on five components, including professional development, compliance with licensing rules and regulations, parent and family involvement, business management, and program assessment. Quality ratings have improved over the 4 years of the program in both centers and family/group homes, with greater improvement in family/group homes noted more recently. Significant improvement in the parent/family involvement scores from Year 1 to Year 4 was found, indicating that family child care providers were more likely to provide an orientation meeting to new families, monthly written communication, opportunities for families to participate in the program, and to offer an annual meeting to review children's progress (University of Tennessee, 2006).

COMMUNITY-BASED APPROACHES—TARGETED TO SPECIFIC PRACTITIONERS/SETTINGS

Family, Friend, and Neighbor Care

Family, friend, and neighbor care (i.e., unregulated care in the home) is a distinct form of care, most often preferred by many families, but challenging to policymakers and researchers because of its unique place in the spectrum of early care and education settings. In 2000, the Families and Work Institute created *Sparking Connections*,[10] a community-based, national initiative designed to support family, friend, and neighbor caregivers (O'Donnell et al., 2006). Driven by the needs of the business community to reduce employee absenteeism due to child care concerns and by the desire of families to place their children in family, friend, and neighbor settings, *Sparking Connections* works in eight communities across the United States to understand the needs of families, employers, and care providers and to develop innovative strategies that help ensure parents have choices of high-quality care that help them balance the demands of work and family.

In 2003, three community-based projects conducted process evaluations over 2 years: the Oklahoma Cherokee Nation Sparking Connections Project, Minnesota Sparking Connections, and the King County, Seattle, Family, Friend, and Neighbor Resource Network. Family support principles, such as viewing children holistically in the context of their families and communities and placing a priority on family needs and desires, that guided program development were found to be critical to reaching goals for both children and families. Significant efforts were focused on building community awareness of the role and value of family, friend, and neighbor care in meeting the needs of families, children, and employers and resulted in increased resources for the provision of services and increased leadership skills of caregivers. The Seattle and Oklahoma projects included methodologies to measure increases in caregiver and/or parent knowledge of child development and resources and activities to support children's healthy development and school readiness. The Oklahoma project had a specific goal of strengthening Cherokee culture and family connections. Each of the projects reported a positive impact on project-specific indicators of child and family well-being (O'Donnell et al., 2006).

Head Start and Early Head Start

The Head Start program gives grants to local public and private non-profit and for-profit agencies to provide comprehensive child development services to economically disadvantaged children and families. Family involvement is a key element in local Head Start and Early Head Start programs and has focused on efforts to encourage families and staff to share decision making about how families and other community agencies support Head Start and Early Head Start programs (e.g., Parent Advisory Council). The Head Start program also provides families with training and education to foster their understanding of and involvement in the development of their children. In the early 1990s a 3-year project was conducted to evaluate the delivery of Head Start services in family child care home settings as compared to traditional center classroom settings.[11] Overall, findings indicated that children in both family child care homes and center-based settings performed similarly and that parent outcomes did not differ significantly by setting. However, differences in family involvement practices based on the setting were found. For example, family child care providers were more likely to identify and document family social service needs, but less likely to offer the range of family involvement practices identified in the program standards. Furthermore, families with children in the family child care setting had more informal contact with providers and were less likely to either feel their help was wanted or to receive training on how to be involved with the activities of the family child care setting; but were more likely to be employed or in school (U.S. Department of Health and Human Services, 2000).

Early Head Start, serving infants and toddlers, encourages home-based delivery of services and offers home visits as part of the program. A recent study by Raikes and colleagues (2006) examined the role of family involvement in home visiting and the implications for child and family outcomes. Raikes identified three components—quality, quantity, and content—of home visiting that had varying impacts on parent involvement practices and child outcomes. The *quantity* of involvement (i.e., duration, intensity) predicted improvement in home language and literacy environments when children were 3 years old; and the *content* of the visit (i.e., focused on the activities of the child) predicted children's cognitive and language development, measures of parental support for children's learning and development, and measures of the home environment as a support for children's learning. Clearly, well-designed and intentional home visiting programs have important implications for family involvement practices. This unique service delivery design offers real promise for learning more about how families and caregivers interact and work in partnership to support the development of young children.

IMPLICATIONS FOR FAMILY AND COMMUNITY PARTNERSHIPS

New understandings of the prevalence, characteristics, and choices that families make in the years before formal schooling, particularly regarding home-based care, continue to evolve. Research is emerging to guide practice in supporting all the adults (in various roles) who care for and facilitate the development of young children. As this chapter has outlined, the implications for renewed focus on, and rigor of, the role of family and community partnerships in supporting children and families in home-based care is great. In this final section, implications for practice and future directions for research are identified.

Implications for Practice

We know from decades of research that the adult–child relationship is paramount to healthy development and readiness for learning (Shonkoff & Phillips, 2000). We know that family involvement (including parenting and parent-provider relationships) supports children's learning and development (Harvard Family Research Project, 2006). What we don't know—yet— are the specific mechanisms and practices by which the relationship between home-based providers and families contribute to the healthy development of both children and families.

Some fundamental issues that will define and shape the "face" of family and community partnerships in home-based care are identified below. For example, family involvement is an ill-defined construct as applied to home-based care and the lack of a clear construct impedes program development and implementation, as well as identification of effective practices. Furthermore, typical family involvement practices have originated in center-based programs and may not be effectively adapted to home-based settings. Little research has identified the specific strategies that most effectively support children's development and learning in a home-based setting and support the caregiver–parent relationship. Home-based practitioners are a highly diverse group, in terms of education, experience, cultural/philosophical beliefs on childrearing, and family involvement and, in general, have not had adequate training on family involvement practices. These fundamental issues impact research, policy, and practice and must be co-constructed by families, practitioners, community members, and other stakeholders in order to meaningfully build the knowledge base and guide practice in the future (Lopez, Kreider, & Caspe, 2005).

The term "family involvement" or even family partnerships may not adequately capture or describe the unique relationships and opportunities for supporting children's development when applied to home-based care. Families choosing home-based care do so based on a particular set of beliefs and needs, and may view home-based providers as an extension of the family with much more fluid boundaries and expectations of the role of adults in caring for children. Home-based providers often do not see themselves as "teachers" or even as "professionals" and for those reasons our traditional approaches to professional development or training on family involvement with these populations may miss the mark because of a lack of understanding of the role of home-based care for families. Terminology issues permeate, and may even create barriers to overall goals of improving the quality of home-based settings and strategies to ensure children are ready to learn upon school entry. These barriers may be magnified for families from different ethnic backgrounds and for those who do not speak English as a first language.

The field has primarily used a program- (or center or classroom) oriented frame of reference to delineate family "involvement" activities. The characteristics of care in the home—which has fewer children, less physical space, and other challenges related to time, transportation, and other issues—do not readily accommodate traditional family involvement practices. Typically family involvement practices have been defined in the research to include activities such as attending parent meetings, parent–staff communications, or families volunteering in the classroom. Defining practices from either a center-based care perspective or adapted from K–12 family involvement approaches may serve to alienate or create unnecessary chasms in the parent–provider relationship.

However, more recent research has sought to understand other features of quality care and their implications for practice, including family involvement practices (Ceglowski & Bacigalupa, 2002). Research on parent perspectives of quality indicate that personal characteristics of the provider, staff responsiveness to family needs (including flexibility of care hours), and frequency of parent–caregiver communication are important to parents' views of quality (Ceglowski & Bacigalupa, 2002; Hofferth et al., 1991). For example, some providers identify a "Parent Corner," a space designated in their home for information and communication with families. Others may use daily journals (particularly to note infant feeding and sleep patterns). Families and providers are in more frequent phone contact throughout the day than center-based providers, which can facilitate communication.

A recent national survey of parents also suggests that families may be most compelled to become involved and/or strengthen involvement when the focus is on how the quality of the early care setting impacts children's brain development, speech development, and enables children to achieve their full potential in school and in life (National Association of Child Care Resource & Referral Agencies, 2006a). Other research has looked at family involvement around literacy practices and found positive results and approaches (Lin, 2003), although this research has primarily focused on practitioners in center-based settings. However, these findings suggest that strategies to engage families and home-based practitioners that are tied directly to supporting children's development and learning may be most effective for partnering with families. For example, some home-based providers may organize field trips that include families or may use family members as a substitute or assistant provider. Most home-based providers have an open-door policy and family members more freely stop in to visit at any time during the day than in center-based settings.

Home-based caregivers are a heterogeneous group, including a range of educational backgrounds, experience, and views of their role. Methods of professional development, training, and other supports for the range of practitioners must consider these characteristics and unique needs. Clarifying and valuing the role that home-based practitioners play in supporting parental choice of care, as well as goals related to the family as a whole and individuals within the family, must underlay the field's theoretical assumptions and approaches to family and community involvement. For example, home-based providers have less time to interact with other providers during the day, so evening or weekend "support group" type meetings are often the only way that family child care providers have the opportunity to get and receive information and discuss issues related to their practice with their peers. Family child care provider networks or other approaches that bring training or information to the provider, in their home or a very convenient local setting, are more likely to be successful since home-based providers typically work 10- to 12-hour days (Hamm, Gault, & Jones-DeWeever, 2005).

Family, friend, and neighbor providers in Washington State were found to prefer receiving information via newsletters, booklets, or tip sheets as well as having access to equipment and resources, such as toys or play kits (Brandon et al., 2002).

Future Directions for Research

Research on home-based care is at a nascent stage and has primarily focused on descriptive studies to understand the prevalence, use, and characteristics of the families and children in home-based care. The role of family involvement in children's learning and development is well documented (Harvard Family Research Project, 2006). However, the specific mechanisms by which home-based caregivers influence family involvement have not been clearly articulated as yet. Researchers are beginning to identify specific pathways by which the provider–parent relationship, and various processes of family involvement, are theorized to impact children's development (Weiss, 2005/2006). More recently, evaluations of specific programs or approaches to improving the overall quality of home-based care are emerging. Studies of the early care and education system that include home-based care settings are also elucidating some of the specific processes and impacts of these settings on children, families, and communities. For the most part, research has been atheoretical or grounded in practice, though more recently research is beginning to focus on specific theories, such as family support principles, family-centered care, and/or family systems theory as a framework to guide program development and research.

New research emanating from the child welfare field, focusing on family-strengthening approaches to preventing child abuse and neglect, may also yield useful constructs for application to understanding family and community involvement in home-based care. Family involvement is defined as "a deliberate and sustained effort to ensure that parents have the necessary opportunities, relationships, networks, and supports to raise their children successfully" by the Family Strengthening Policy Center (National Human Services Assembly, 2004). Recent research is beginning to identify family involvement approaches of child and youth program models that impact specific parenting and child outcomes (Caspe & Lopez, 2006). The next generation of research will allow the field to probe deeper on the specific definitions of family and community involvement applicable to home-based care settings and to identify the specific practices of family and community involvement that lead to positive outcomes for children and families.

SUMMARY

Home-based care, the oldest and most prevalent form of care for many American children, is also one of the more difficult types of care to describe and study. Because home-based care is so closely aligned with family responsibilities and preference, and is most often outside the jurisdiction of government regulation, the field has only just begun to understand the implications of this form of care for the well-being of children, and the role it might play in strengthening family, school, and community partnerships. Policymakers, driven by federal funding to support low-income working families and with a focus on supporting children's school readiness, are addressing home-based care within quality improvement efforts for the early care and education system. Researchers are beginning to place more emphasis on theory-driven approaches to study the impact of the features of caregiving in homes that make a difference. In order to provide families with the flexibility and range of care options to meet their needs, it is critical that the field continues to focus research and policy on the role of home-based care in strengthening family involvement in children's learning, and the roles of communities in partnering with families and other key stakeholders to improve the quality of home-based settings.

ACKNOWLEDGMENTS

The authors thank the Child Care Bureau, Office of Family Assistance, Administration for Children and Families, U.S. Department of Health and Human Services, and the National Child Care Information and Technical Assistance Center, a service of the Child Care Bureau, for their guidance and support in writing this chapter. The authors appreciate the contributions of Ivelisse Martinez-Beck, PhD, Child Care Research Coordinator, Office of Planning, Research and Evaluation, for her ideas and suggestions in conceptualizing the chapter.

NOTES

1. The contents of this chapter are solely the responsibility of the authors and do not represent the official view of the Child Care Bureau, the Administration for Children and Families, or the U.S. Department of Health and Human Services, nor does publication in any way constitute endorsement by these agencies.
2. Individuals hired by the family to care for the children in their own home.
3. The Bureau of Labor Statistics (BLS) collects data on "child care workers," which include some home-based caregivers, nannies, and family child care

home assistants—but not owners of family child care homes who are the actual caregiver (Brandon & Martinez-Beck, 2005). Family child care providers and in-home workers are included in Census Bureau data, but neither Census nor BLS data include family, friend, and neighbor caregivers, who are the majority of individuals who provide home-based care.

4. See the National Child Care Information Center's Child Care Licensing Requirements: Minimum Early Childhood Education (ECE) Preservice Qualifications, Orientation/Initial Licensure, and Annual Ongoing Training Hours for Family Child Care Providers for more information (http://nccic.acf.hhs.gov/pubs/cclicensingreq/cclr-famcare.html)

5. Child Care and Development Fact Sheet (October 2006), http://www.acf.hhs.gov/programs/ccb/ccdf/factsheet.htm

6. For more information on the Child Development Associate credential, including the requirements for achieving the credential, see http://www.cda-council.org.

7. Visit the National Resource Center for Health and Safety in Child Care and Early Education Web site for additional information about and a national overview of State child care licensing regulations at http://nrc.uchsc.edu/STATES/states.htm.

8. Federal block grants are "fixed-sum federal grants to state and local governments that give them broad flexibility to design and implement designated programs." For more information, see http://www.urban.org/publications/310991.html.

9. Early learning guidelines define what children should know, understand, and be able to do upon entry to kindergarten. States use a variety of terms, such as *content standards, benchmarks,* or *framework,* in the title of the state-developed document. For further information, see http://nccic.org/pubs/goodstart/framework-quality.html.

10. For more information on Sparking Connections, please visit http://www.familiesandwork.org/sparking/home.htm.

11. For more information about Head Start's home-based option, please visit Part 1306: Head Start Staffing Requirements and Program Option of the Head Start Program Performance Standards, http://eclkc.ohs.acf.hhs.gov/hslc.

REFERENCES

Adams, G., Tout, K., & Zaslow, M. (2007). *Early care and education for children in low-income families: Patterns of use, quality, and potential policy implications.* Washington, DC: Urban Institute and Child Trends.

American Public Human Services Association (APHSA) and Child Trends. (2006, April).

Investing in quality: A survey of state Child Care and Development Fund initiatives. Washington, DC: Author.

Anderson, S., Ramsburg, D., & Scott, J. (2005). *Illinois study of license-exempt child care: Final report.* Springfield: Illinois Department of Human Services.

Annie E. Casey Foundation. (2006). *Family, friend, and neighbor care: Strengthening a critical resource to help young children succeed (Kids Count essay).* Baltimore: Author.

Atkinson, A. (1994). Rural and urban families' use of child care. *Family Relations, 43*(1), 16–22.

Brandon, R. (2005). *Enhancing family, friend and neighbor caregiving quality: The research case for public engagement.* Washington, DC: American Public Human Services Association. Retrieved August 22, 2005, from http://www.aphsa.org/Publications/Doc/Brandon-Family-Friend-and-Neighbor-Paper.pdf

Brandon, R., Maher, E., Joesch, J., & Doyle, S. (2002, February). *Understanding family, friend, and neighbor care in Washington State: Developing appropriate training and support.* Retrieved September 17, 2006, from http://hspc.org/publications/understanding_family.aspx

Brandon, R. N., & Martinez-Beck, I. (2005). Estimating the size and characteristics of the U.S. early care and education workforce. In M. Zaslow & I. Martinez-Beck (Eds.), *Critical issues in early childhood professional development.* Baltimore: Paul H. Brookes..

Butler, J., Bringham, N., & Schultheiss, S. (1991). *No place like home: A study of subsidized in-home and relative child day care.* Philadelphia: Rosenblum and Associates.

Caspe, M., & Lopez, M.E. (October, 2006). *Lessons from family-strengthening interventions: Learning from evidence-based practice.* Cambridge, MA: Harvard Family Research Project, Harvard Graduate School of Education.

Ceglowski, D. & Bacigalupa, C. (2002). Four perspectives on child care quality. *Early Childhood Education Journal, 30*(2), 87–92.

Center for the Child Care Workforce and the Human Services Policy Center. (2002). *Estimating the size and components of the U.S. child care workforce and caregiving population.* Washington, DC, and Seattle, WA: Authors.

Child Care Bureau. (2006). *Child Care and Development Fund Report of State Plans FY 2004-2005.* Washington, DC: U.S. Department of Health and Human Services, Administration for Children and Families, Child Care Bureau.

Child Care Bureau. (2005). *FFY 2005 Child Care Development Fund data tables (preliminary estimates).* Washington, DC: U.S. Department of Health and Human Services, Administration for Children and Families, Child Care Bureau.

Coley, R., Chase-Lansdale, P.L., & Li-Grining, C. (2001). *Child care in the era of welfare reform: Quality, choices, and preferences* (Policy Brief 01-04). Baltimore: Johns Hopkins University.

Edie, D. (2006). *Toward a new child care policy.* Washington, DC: The Urban Institute.

Galinsky, E., Howes, C., Kontos, S., & Shinn, M. (1994). *The study of children in family child care and relative care: Highlights of findings.* New York: Families and Work Institute.

Green, B.L., McAllister, C.L., & Tarte, J.M. (2004). The strengths-based practices inventory: A tool for measuring strengths-based service delivery in early childhood and family support programs. *Families in Society, 85,* 326–334.

Hamm, K., Gault, B., & Jones-DeWeever, A. (2005). *In our own backyards: Local and state strategies to improve the quality of family child care.* Washington, DC: Institute for Women's Policy Research.

Harvard Family Research Project. (2006). *Family involvement makes a difference: Evidence that family involvement promotes school success for every child of every age.* Cambridge, MA: Harvard Graduate School of Education.

Hertz, R., & Ferguson, F. (1996). Child care choice and constraints in the United States: Social class, race and the influence of family views. *Journal of Comparative Family Studies, 27*(2), 249–280.

Hofferth, S., Brayfield, A., Deitch, S., & Holcomb, P. (1991). *National Child Care Survey, 1990.* Washington, DC: Urban Institute Press.

Iruka, I. U., & Carver, P. R. (2006). *Initial results from the 2005 NHES Early Childhood Program Participation Survey* (NCES 2006-075). Washington, DC: National Center for Education Statistics.

Johnson, J. (2005). *Who's minding the kids? Child care arrangements: Winter 2002.* Washington, DC: U.S. Census Bureau.

Layzer, J., & Goodson, B. (2006). *Care in the home: A description of family child care and the experiences of the families and children that use it* (National Study of Child Care for Low-Income Families, Wave I Report). Cambridge, MA: Abt Associates.

Lin, Q. (2003). *Research digest: Parent involvement and early literacy.* Cambridge, MA: Harvard Family Research Project.

Lopez, E., Kreider, H., & Caspe, M. (2005). Co-constructing family involvement. *Evaluation Exchange, X*(4). Cambridge, MA: Harvard Family Research Project.

Maxwell, K. (2005, April). *Legal, nonregulated care in North Carolina.* Paper presented at the Society for Research in Child Development Biennial Meeting, Atlanta, GA.

Mensing, J., French, D., Fuller, B., & Kagan, S. (2000). Child care selection under welfare reform: How mothers balance work requirements and parenting. *Early Education and Development, 11,* 573–595.

Mitchell, A. (2005b). *Success stories: State investments in early care and education in Illinois, North Carolina and Rhode.* Greensboro, NC: Smart Start Technical Assistance Center.

Mitchell, A. (2005a). *Stair steps to quality: A guide for states and communities developing Quality Rating Systems for early care and education.* Fairfax, VA: Caliber & United Way of America Success by 6.

Mitchell, A., & Lemoine, S. (2005). *Cross-sector early childhood professional development.* Fairfax, VA: National Child Care Information Center. Retrieved September 15, 2006, from http://nccic.acf.hhs.gov/pubs/goodstart/cross-sector.pdf

National Association of Child Care Resource & Referral Agencies. (2006b). *State child care resource and referral networks.* Arlington, VA: Author.

National Association of Child Care Resource & Referral Agencies. (2006a). *Parents' perceptions of child care in the United States: NACCRRA's national parent poll.* Arlington, VA: Author.

National Child Care Information Center. (2007, April). *Quality rating systems: Definitions and statewide systems.* Fairfax, VA: Author. Retrieved June 26, 2007, from http://nccic.acf.hhs.gov/pubs/qrs-defsystems.html

National Child Care Information Center. (2005, June). *Common categories of criteria used in state quality rating systems.* Fairfax, VA: Author. Retrieved September 15, 2006, from http://nccic.acf.hhs.gov/pubs/qrs-comcat.pdf

National Human Services Assembly. (2004, October). *Introduction to family strengthening* (Policy Brief No. 1). Washington, DC: Author. Retrieved August 7, 2007, from http://www.nassembly.org/fspc/practice/documents/Brief1.pdf

National Institute of Child Health and Human Development Early Child Care Research Network. (2007). Are there long-term effects of early child care? *Child Development, 78*(2), 681–701.

O'Donnell, N., Cochran, M., Lekies, K., Diehl, D., Morrissey, T., Ashley, N. et al. (2006). *Sparking Connections: A multi-site evaluation of community-based strategies to support family, friend, and neighbor caregivers of children, Phase II: Lessons learned and recommendations.* New York: Families and Work Institute.

Porter, T., & Kearns, S. (2005). *Supporting family, friend and neighbor care: Findings from a survey of state policies.* New York: Institute for a Child Care Continuum, Bank Street College of Education.

Porter, T., & Rice, R. (2000). *Lessons learned: Strategies for working with kith and kin caregivers.* New York: Bank Street College of Education.

Raikes, H., Green, B., Atwater, J., Kisker, E., Constantine, J. & Chazan-Cohen, R. (2006). Involvement in Early Head Start home visiting services: Demographic predictors and relations to child and parent outcomes. *Early Childhood Research Quarterly, 21*, 2–24.

Shonkoff, J., & Phillips, D. (2000). *From neurons to neighborhoods: The science of early childhood development.* Washington, DC: National Academy Press.

Smith, K. (2006). *Rural families choose home-based care for their preschool-aged children.* Policy Brief No. 3, 1-2. Durham: Carsey Institute, University of New Hampshire. Retrieved September, 2006, from http://www.carseyinstitute.unh.edu/documents/ChildCare_final.pdf.

University of Tennessee. (2006). *Tennessee Report Card and Star Quality Program—Year 4 annual report.* Nashville: TN: Author.

U.S. Department of Health and Human Services. (2000). *Evaluation of Head Start Family Child Care Demonstration: Final Report.* Washington, DC: Author.

Weiss, H. (2005/2006, Winter). Pathways from workforce development to child outcomes. *Evaluation Exchange, XI*(4). Retrieved April 3, 2006, from www.gse.harvard.edu/hfrp/eval/issue32/theory.html

CHAPTER 6

WHAT DO FAMILIES WANT?

Understanding their GOALS for Early Childhood Services

Sejal Patel, Carl Corter, and Janette Pelletier

INTRODUCTION

Early childhood professionals concerned with determining if they are meeting child and family needs achieve the most basic level of accountability when they invite family member participation in the process. The importance of family input is widely recognized in policy, often with corresponding practices focusing on governance roles (e.g., Organization for Economic Cooperation and Development, 1997). However, governance is only one avenue for family input and is not sufficient. In many cases, participation in governance only captures the interest of a small minority of families. In fact, if formal governance structures take too much organizational time and effort, they may actually be counterproductive for children's development and learning (Corter & Pelletier, 2005). This chapter emphasizes the need to move beyond governance as a means for seeking family input. Professionals and service organizations need more effective means for knowing "where families are coming from" and must take families' needs and aims into account in designing and delivering early childhood programs and services.

Promising Practices for Partnering with Families in the Early Years, pages 103–135
Copyright © 2008 by Information Age Publishing
All rights of reproduction in any form reserved.

A major goal of the chapter is to describe different channels for hearing from families, channels that apply to any type of early childhood service. By hearing from families, we mean asking families what their goals are as they enter the service and seeking continuing input on service delivery and design. Hearing from families is an important part of the respectful engagement that is needed between services and families. This engagement means a respectful dialogue, not just listening. For example, it can include informing families about service options they may not have thought about. However, in the chapter we emphasize "hearing from families" because this part of engagement has not been a focus in practice or in the literature.

Throughout the chapter we describe multiple strategies for giving families real voice about what their goals are both for their children and for themselves, and ways to meet their diverse needs. This includes establishing relationships between families and professionals as a foundation for hearing from each other and for mutual support in the common goal of promoting children's learning and development. We emphasize a knowledge-building, team approach to practice. Professionals hearing from each other in systematic ways, as well as from families, can build better practice as professional teams target concrete improvements in partnering with families.

Other strategies may also help organizations enhance their effectiveness for children and families. A prime example of an organizational change that can increase families' voice and choice is the seamless integration of services that traditionally operate in separate "silos" such as kindergarten and childcare (Desimone, Payne, Fedoravicius, Henrich, & Finn-Stevenson, 2004). We present service integration as a promising organizational strategy to amplify families' voices and engagement and describe how this works in a school-based hub approach. Families who are able to access services through one entry point are more likely to have their views heard and addressed.

The potential of this model is exemplified in our discussion of the Toronto First Duty demonstration project. Our evaluation of this project reveals that integration of services, in contrast to separate services, makes it easier to hear from families and to meet their needs in supporting their children. We conclude the chapter by summarizing key research findings that early childhood professionals and organizations can use in pursuing families' input, thus improving outcomes for children and families.

FAMILY INVOLVEMENT BENEFITS CHILDREN, FAMILIES, AND PROFESSIONALS

Family or parent[1] involvement is a widely acclaimed principle in preschool programs and schooling. Early childhood services, such as child care and kindergarten, have a long tradition of involving families as part of everyday practice (e.g., National Association for the Education of Young Children, 2004). The potential importance for children's school success has received the lion's share of attention in the literature on benefits of engaging families in education. Numerous correlational studies show improved academic performance when parents are more engaged (Corter & Pelletier, 2005) or when schools are more engaging (e.g., Sheldon, 2003).

However, there are other potential benefits beyond academic achievement for children, families, and professionals. These are particularly apparent in early childhood programs, which by their nature take a whole-child approach and sometimes include family support and education as a prime program focus. For example, our own studies of early childhood services show that involving parents can increase their feelings of efficacy (e.g., Patel & Corter, 2005; Pelletier & Brent, 2002), which may in turn have positive benefits for children's learning and socioemotional development. Professionals report more satisfying relationships with families through experiences in integrated programs and better socioemotional outcomes for children may result from this integrative experience (Corter, Patel, Pelletier, & Bertrand, 2008). Explicit consideration of families' goals can also contribute to relationship building between professionals and families and may result in more engaged and efficacious families (Pelletier & Corter, 2005).

Unfortunately, the potential benefits of family involvement are not always achieved. Programs seeking to boost school achievement by increasing family involvement don't always work (Mattingly, Prislin, McKenzie, Rodriguez, & Kayzar, 2002). Not all types of family involvement are equally effective and not all types of involvement are equally important to different groups of families as distinguished by income levels and cultural differences (e.g., Ho & Willms, 1996). Furthermore, the practice of designing programs and services based on hearing from families is not a pervasive part of current practice, either in early childhood services or schools.

NEW STRATEGIES ARE NEEDED TO HEAR WHAT FAMILIES WANT

Epstein's types of parent–school partnership activities—which include parenting, communication, volunteering, learning at home, decision making, and collaborating with the community (see Epstein & Salinas, 1993)—are now standard ways of thinking about promoting family–school connections starting in kindergarten. Similar categories are found in analyses of early childhood services such as child care and family support programs (e.g., Castro, Bryant, Peisner-Feinberg, & Skinner, 2004). Among Epstein's six types of involvement, family participation in governance and communication between home and school both suggest opportunities to hear from families.

However, both communication and governance participation require structuring and tuning to be effective for finding out about "what families want." Without such attention, communication may be one-sided from school to home and may focus on children without accounting for families' goals. Traditional ways of communicating tend to be one-way and focused on the professional's agenda (Pushor, 2007). Most of the research indicates that simple governance roles do not always give families voice, even for the few who serve in those roles (Seitsinger & Zera, 2002). Furthermore, school councils are not uniformly effective and do not represent families at large (Corter & Pelletier, 2005; Parker & Leithwood, 2000).

In a study across six elementary schools in three school districts where school councils were mandated to give families a voice (Corter, Harris, & Pelletier, 1998), none of the dozens of school council members surveyed were parents of kindergarten children. None of the school council representatives identified themselves as being of visible minority status or reported a first language other than English, although nearly a third of the families in these schools belonged to these groups.

Early childhood programs encounter similar problems. In Head Start, which mandates parent participation in governance, and child care programs in which families serve as members of operating committees, these governance roles may not be effective in representing views of parents at large; the small number of parents who serve in governance roles may be selected or socialized to be compatible with professional views rather than the diversity of parental views (Seitsinger & Zera, 2002). While relationships between early childhood educators and families may benefit from the built-in opportunities for daily family–professional communication during drop-off and pick-up times, miscommunication is possible in these everyday exchanges. For example, culturally diverse families have been shown to have different goals for their children's development than teachers in early childhood settings, including different views about social development and attitudes about respect for authority (Bernhard, Lefebvre, Kilbride, Chud, & Lange, 1998). Furthermore, families and educators are often unaware of their differing goals. This leads to problematic encounters between families and staff and less-than-optimal conditions for children's early education.

Two-way communication is becoming more complicated as early childhood services in many parts of the world struggle to meet the needs of increasingly diverse populations of children and families. In some cases, hearing from families is precluded by problems of access such as underutilization of services by those most in need, or by those who face language or cultural barriers. Specialized services and prevention programs may not include effective outreach strategies to draw in diverse families and their children. In other cases, families may find that programs don't match their needs. Some family involvement interventions designed to close "gaps" for children who are falling behind may actually widen gaps when families of children who are at lower risk participate at higher rates (see Ceci & Papierno, 2005). Despite these challenges, efforts to involve families in early childhood services continue to grow because of global social forces ranging from pressures for accountability and democratic participation (Corter & Pelletier, 2005), to new "community" models of service provision (Anderson-Parsons, 1997).

To be effective, better communication is needed. True family involvement can only take place when communication and information exchange occur in a reciprocal manner because, after all, "listening to parents, is just as important as giving instructions and passing on important information about the schooling process" (Bhering, 2002, p. 235). Furthermore, we argue that families' goals must be taken into account: what families want for their children and what they hope to accomplish through their own involvement in the process.

WHAT ARE FAMILIES' GOALS AND WHAT ARE THE BENEFITS OF TAKING THEM INTO ACCOUNT?

Parents have diverse needs and goals when they access early childhood services. Although they are most often concerned with their children's social development and readiness for school learning, families also have goals for themselves, ranging from being part of a group to becoming better parents.

Parents' goals can be thought of as falling within two categories: child-oriented goals and self-oriented goals; each of these can be broken into two subcategories (Dix, 1992). According to Dix (1992), the two subcategories of child-oriented parenting goals are empathy and socialization. Empathy-related goals involve giving the child what he or she "wants." Examples include playing with the child, being sensitive to the child's needs, and striving to satisfy the child's wishes. Socialization-related goals involve giving the child what the parent thinks that he or she "needs." Examples of socialization goals include families' discipline activities, attempts to promote the social and cognitive development of their children, and the direct instruction of skills. In contrast to these child-oriented parenting goals, self-oriented goals aim to improve the adult's life as a parent, without the intention of directly influencing the life of their child (Dix, 1992). These include families' desires for affiliation, achievement, and power.

Goals are important precursors for concrete behaviors (Pervin, 1989) and parenting goals have been posited to relate to children's outcomes. In all of these cases, that is, parents' goals to meet their child's interests or their own interests, it is important for early childhood professionals to be in tune with families' goals for accessing services in order to appropriately gear their practices toward collaboration. This is especially true when early childhood programs aim to provide parent support as well as child development support.

A study by Bettler and Burns (2003) found that families' parenting goals were significant predictors of cognitive development in a sample of 220 children from families with low incomes and significant predictors of grade 1 school readiness in a retrospective study with a sample of 290 middle-class college students. This suggests that families' goals in accessing early childhood services have an impact on their children's development. According to Darling and Steinberg (1993), children's developmental and socialization outcomes originate from families' attitudes and behaviors (parenting style and practices), which develop from parenting goals and values. Thus, child-oriented parenting goals can be an excellent leverage point for interventions aimed specifically at improving parental involvement (Bettler & Burns, 2003), and for early childhood programs and services in general.

Being aware of families' goals brings added benefits. A goal-based approach to early childhood services facilitates two-way communication between families and professionals, which may help to encourage more culturally sensitive communication and to avoid deficit assumptions by professionals about the families they are working with (Bettler & Burns, 2003). This may help to increase family involvement of otherwise marginalized families.

Goals stemming from different types of parental involvement (i.e., Epstein's partnership activities) in early childhood services may be more meaningful for some families than others, depending on family circumstances (Patel, 2004). Parents vary in how they want to be involved in their children's services. Volunteering and committee work aren't necessarily for everyone. Fostering different types of involvement supports collaboration between families and teachers because families can choose the path that works for them (Cairney & Munsie, 1995).

STRATEGIES FOR DETERMINING FAMILIES' NEEDS AND GOALS

Professionals can determine families' needs and goals for seeking early childhood services upon initial intake into programs and services, through informal interviews (i.e., just talking to families), surveys (e.g., Bettler, 2001), and focus groups (e.g., Stiles, 2005). Ideally, these goal assessments can guide the direction of future program and service participation to ensure that families are getting what they want, not just what professionals think that they need.

An example of the direction we are advocating is taken from a study of exemplary kindergartens we conducted some years ago (Corter & Park, 1993). An outstanding teacher we interviewed said she begins the school year with a parent interview. She opened each interview with an invitation to "tell me about your theory of education." Her aim was to hear parents' goals for their children and to recognize the parents' right to have ideas. It is important to note, however, that these interviews involved two-way communication with learning on both sides of the exchange. After hearing from the parents, the teacher went on to share what she believes are the goals of kindergarten and how goals are individualized according to her understanding of each child. A respectful interchange includes sharing information about each child. This teacher recognized that parents have unique knowledge of their children that should be considered in programming. She also believed that it is important to hear about their goals, recognize areas where views of teacher and parent might differ, and to find common ground for the year ahead.

SHARING PROFESSIONAL KNOWLEDGE WITH FAMILIES

As suggested above, hearing from families shouldn't be a passive exercise; professionals in the early childhood field, including policy analysts and researchers, have a responsibility to share knowledge. As part of respectful exchanges, families deserve balanced information about service options and quality issues in different kinds of services. Of course, there is a delicate balance between overpowering families with communications from the professional side and assessing what families bring to the table outside of managed interchanges (Pushor, 2007). Families may not necessarily have knowledge about early childhood services and what the literature shows to be important for optimizing children's development and offering family support. Research suggests that the media do not help in this regard (Kunkel, Smith, Siding, & Biely, 2006); newspaper and television reports rarely deal with issues of quality or effectiveness of early childhood programs and policy.

Research also suggests that families are limited in their abilities to judge the quality of child care and need help in recognizing what good early childhood service really is (Cryer, Tietze, & Wessels, 2002). And our own research shows that families and communities are not aware of new options such as integrated services or flexible child care (Corter et al., 2006). These findings reveal a gap between what the public actually knows about early childhood services and what professionals say is important for children's development and for family support. What can be done about this gap?

Part of the solution may lie in Sharon Kagan's (1999) suggestion that professional training in early childhood should include learning how to advocate for the field itself, with the public and policymakers. In the meantime, professionals can get started on sharing their knowledge about quality and how they implement practices that manifest it. As they introduce new and effective strategies they can invite families "inside" the program to see it in action and to get a firsthand sense of how success is measured. As one example, Souto-Manning and Lee (2005) showed that families can become more accepting of play as a program medium when they are shown how play can be structured to produce results through a project approach to learning. Portfolios of children's play activities and products can be markers of progress and eye-openers when they are shared with parents.

A KNOWLEDGE-BUILDING APPROACH
TO WORK WITH FAMILIES

At an organizational level we need to hear from families about what they want, we need to share what we know, and we need to build the shared understanding into action. Knowledge building is an approach that makes knowledge improvement the goal (Pelletier, Reeve, & Halewood, 2006); it can be applied to any organization, from classrooms to service organizations. To apply this to the present discussion, the collaborative goal is to improve practitioners' knowledge about what individual families want and to improve family knowledge about the goals and methods of practitioners. In addition, a collaborative goal for parents and professionals is to build understanding of individual children and general child development and learning.

For practitioners in early childhood programs or schools, knowledge building to improve ideas for practice and programs is facilitated by "communities of practice" (Wenger, 2001). A community of practice is a group of people who share a common concern or enthusiasm about a topic, and who deepen their expertise and knowledge by interacting on an ongoing basis (Snyder, Wenger, & Briggs, 2004). Professionals in a community of practice connect to develop relationships with peers and stakeholders, solve problems, build tools together, and share ideas and a common passion regarding a particular practice domain. In this case, communities of practice include professionals and families who share goals and knowledge, leading to sustained improvement in services for children.

According to Wenger (2004, p. 6), "the most successful communities have always combined bottom-up enthusiasm and initiative from members with top-down encouragement from the organization." Communities of practice are an effective means of crossing boundaries within and between organizations to engage in interdisciplinary knowledge building.

STRATEGIES FOR KNOWLEDGE BUILDING
IN PROFESSIONAL DEVELOPMENT

The effectiveness of a community of practice depends on the strength of three structural dimensions of the community (Wenger, 2000): the domain (focal issue), the community (quality of relationships/interactions between members), and practice (repertoire of tools, methods, and learning and innovation activities. According to Wenger (2004), professionals need to form communities in their own domain, and then mutual engagement needs to be supported through a process of practice development, not simply one-shot brown bag lunches about a topic or issue. Professionals need opportunities to engage directly with one another and to share the challenges they're facing and how they are approaching these problems. Community participation needs to be directly relevant to the work of community members (Wenger, 2004). For example, if a new solution is proposed in a practice community, professionals can apply this to their own work and vice versa; if a new solution is discovered by a community member in their work, they can share it with the community of practice (Wenger, 2004). An important aspect of a community of practice is dissemination; lessons learned and best practices that arise from the work of a community of practice should be shared (Wenger, 2004). A key element of a successful community of practice is an appropriate leadership infrastructure that can guide, renew, and support (Snyder et al., 2004) the community of practice over time. A community coordinator is a helpful role to create within a community of practice (Snyder et al., 2004). Communities of practice can meet face to face, or virtually through online discussions.

SERVICE INTEGRATION AS A
FAMILY INVOLVEMENT STRATEGY

At the level of organizational change, service integration is another promising practice for hearing from families and for serving them and their children better. There are numerous reasons why integrating preschool services at school sites might open more channels for hearing from families and for involving them in other ways. First, multiple services allow a "menu" of choices for engaging a wider range of families. When child care and kindergarten are combined, as in Edward Zigler's Schools of the 21st Century approach, there is greater continuity for parents as well as for children (Finn-Stevenson, Desimone, & Chung, 1998). Parents' relationships formed with child care professionals may enhance those with kindergarten teachers and vice versa (Desimone et al., 2004). The relatively positive views that parents have toward child care (e.g., Cryer et al., 2002) as compared to other services may benefit the school in a setting where child care and school are integrated. When parenting support services are included in the mix, the direct benefits of parent education may be accompanied by more positive parental attitudes and feelings of efficacy that generalize to relationships with child services and the school (Pelletier & Brent, 2002). Improved relationships have the potential to provide more effective opportunities to understand parents' goals. Finally, when these integrated services are offered in the school, there is greater opportunity for a wider range of professionals to hear what parents want.

THE TORONTO FIRST DUTY EXAMPLE

So far, we have argued that professionals should conduct goal assessments as families come into contact with early childhood services and that they should help families understand their alternatives so that families make choices according to their own needs and goals. Sharing professional knowledge with families is an important part of professionals' work and sharing practical knowledge with one another is an important part of professional development. Improved relationships between families and professionals and within professional groups allow ongoing opportunities for respectful interactions and dialogue between families and professionals.

We have studied these strategies as part of demonstration projects offering universally available integrated services, supporting the transition to school in the greater Toronto region, a culturally and linguistically diverse urban area (see Pelletier & Corter, 2006). One ambitious early integrated services initiative we have studied is the Toronto First Duty (TFD) project (for overviews, see Corter et al., 2006; Pelletier & Corter, 2006). The TFD initiative was based on broad child development and parenting support goals and a vision of universally available, integrated services to achieve the goals. Demonstration sites were established at five schools. At each site, the model called for an integrated, universally available service core consisting of child care, school kindergarten, and parent education programs. Other community services, such as public health and child and family mental health, also joined in the integrated service mix. Each site was to work toward deep integration along dimensions of a common learning environment, a united early childhood staff team, seamless access, integrated governance, and common family outreach and involvement strategies. Parents were free to choose which aspects of the integrated service mix they and their children would take up, although almost all 4- and 5-year old children at the five sites attended half-day kindergarten whether or not they participated in other services.

Evaluation included summative reporting on the project at the end of 4 years as well as formative feedback to sites throughout the course of the project. The project also included an intake and tracking system providing continuous quantitative monitoring of program intake and participation. The system was a City of Toronto administrative database that provided both accountability information and formative feedback to the five demonstration sites. The database includes information over a 3-year period on 2,643 children and their parents who participated across the five sites.

Determining Families' Goals

Families completed an intake form asking questions relating to their demographic characteristics as well as descriptions of their goals and experiences in utilizing programs and services (Corter et al., 2006). Specifically, the intake form asked questions such as, "What are your program goals?"; "What programs and services have you accessed previously?"; and "How would you like to participate in this program?"; with a checklist for families to select options from. For the question regarding families' program goals, possible responses were, "access child care," "be part of a group," "do fun things," "have a chance for a break," "access special services," "learn more about parenting," "positive discipline," "support child's development," "meet other children," and "prepare for school," among others.

Most families reported multiple goals in connecting to the service array. Parents typically had goals for themselves as well as for their children. In fact, 81% had more than one goal for their children and 64% of families had more than one goal for themselves. In general, goals for children outweighed the goals parents had for themselves. The foremost goals for children were opportunities for meeting other children (73%), enhancing child development (65%), doing fun things (63%), and promoting school readiness (61%). The foremost goals for parenting to improve children's development were learning about positive discipline (50%) and learning more about parenting (50%). The highest-ranking goals for parents themselves were to be part of a group (50%), accessing child care (34%), and having a break (34%).

We also looked at families' interest in various forms of "family involvement" as they came into the project. The data show that many were ready to be involved in a variety of ways, ranging from taking part in special events (59%), organizing special events (38%), and volunteering (34%), to being a committee member (33%).

Moving away from general interests, we looked at families' goals for their children by asking about their "concerns" as well as their positive aims. The most commonly reported concerns for their children were related to speech and language, with 42% of parents reporting this concern (note that 57% of the parents did not speak English as a first language), and 27% of parents reported "behavioral" concerns.

Families Experiences with Services

Families' reports of their experiences with the TFD integrated service approach were drawn from focus groups and surveys with families. Surveys were translated into five additional languages, including Bengali, Cantonese, Mandarin, Tamil, and Vietnamese. While a translation option was offered for focus groups across sites, none of the participants requested translation. The data indicated high levels of family/client satisfaction with the TFD services. Among the positive comments families stated "very satisfied"; "the most positive is that the children come here and it prepares them for kindergarten"; "I feel it's my house. We know each other...like family." Focus group results were mirrored in the survey data. For example, 97% of parents surveyed agreed, or strongly agreed, that "Toronto First Duty helps my child get ready for school socially." TFD families also endorsed the idea of integrated services significantly more than parents in communities without TFD, suggesting that families are less likely to want what they don't know.

Despite the general satisfaction during early implementation, the surveys and focus group probing showed that families felt that they weren't part of the planning for programs. In response to a question about family input into programming, participants tended to agree with one parent's focus group comment, "Nobody asked us." This was true despite formal parental representation on site steering committees and the use of intake information about families' goals in tailoring programs. Nevertheless, most families felt they personally had no input.

This perspective surprised the sites. Given that the research team and their own informal information collection showed that families liked the program, this information from families opened everyone's eyes to the need to "ask all parents what they want." Although sites had held initial community consultations, they had involved only a small sample of families and these consultations were not ongoing. On the intake forms, families weren't asked about the service array, timing, or design. They were only asked about their goals for an existing array of services, not regarding the actual service design. Ideally, families should be consulted on an ongoing basis about service design and delivery with accommodations where possible.

Another negative comment concerned the lack of flexibility in program times or content, and the lack of availability of some programs at some sites. This information was revealed through the site-level surveys completed by families. It is important to note that had they not been prompted by the survey to consider issues of flexibility and availability; these views may not have been expressed spontaneously.

Although the earlier findings on TFD families' views on services in general were quite positive, sites worked to improve family engagement throughout the implementation period based on feedback on areas where there were more mixed results: ability to access services and being asked about their opinions on services. Comparisons of early implementation to full implementation demonstrated further improvements. In particular, over time, significantly more families reported feeling that their opinion is valued and that teachers/staff ask their opinion about programs and services, in comparison to family reports during early implementation. Furthermore, families during later implementation were significantly less likely to report that they haven't been able to use the programs/services for children/families in comparison to family reports during early implementation.

These findings point to the usefulness of employing a multimethod approach to gathering families' views. Organizations can profit from having a variety of ways to hear from families: channels such as focus group meetings with food, simple surveys, intake and evaluation forms, or simply having informal conversations with parents.

Responding to Family Feedback

Staff teams at each site heard the feedback from families and made a variety of adjustments. Teams of early childhood staff, family support workers, and kindergarten teachers worked together with families' input in mind to boost weekend and summer opportunities for program participation. Staff reviewed regular reports of participation rates to monitor demand. Resources were regularly reallocated across the range of programs to meet family demand as indexed by participation. An example of directly responding to family input was one site's effort to engage families who indicated via the intake and tracking process that they had an interest in committee work.

Over the implementation of TFD, survey reports across sites began to reflect these positive changes. Although there was still room for improvement, families increasingly felt that they were being heard and that there was better access to services.

Knowledge Building for Program Improvement

As researchers, we used a knowledge-building evaluation approach that allowed us to join TFD partners and frontline staff in a community of practice, for the purpose of project improvement. In addition to examining ongoing intake and tracking information, we collected feedback from focus group and survey data over time and conveyed our findings to the sites. Frontline staff and site leaders reflected on the information about what families wanted and made changes. A number of sites systematically collected family views of various program elements. The change in survey reports showed that parents increasingly felt that they were "being listened to" and that there was greater "availability of services." Our research team also developed a tool that assisted site teams in periodic self-assessment on key dimensions of moving toward service integration (the First Duty Indicators of Change tool; Corter et al., 2006). This tool describes progress toward integration on a continuum of change that includes coexistence, coordination, collaboration, and integration as benchmarks. The indicators describe levels of integration for five dimensions: programming, staff teamwork, seamless access, governance, and parent–community involvement. In the tool, incremental steps for improving family input are laid out for a number of subdimensions: family input into program decisions, family participation in programs, parenting capacity, and relationships with families. Sites identified where they were on the Indicators of Change continuum, using their direct experience and research information, and made plans for improvement.

We provided formative feedback and assistance with the Indicators of Change self-assessment as part of case studies at each of the five sites. The case studies were based on mixed methods to describe and analyze the development, implementation, and potential effects of the TFD program across the 4 years of the project. The data collection included meeting notes and other records from site agencies; participant observation in organizational meetings, including some integrated staff team meetings; key informant interviews with site leaders; focus groups and interviews with program staff, parents, and children; and surveys with parents and staff. An important conclusion from the case studies is that *time* for staff to meet together and reflect on ideas, actions, and results is crucial for success, allowing information to be turned into shared knowledge and effective action.

The other side of knowledge building was what parents learned; knowledge building worked both ways. Families learned about services (e.g., outreach and learning about availability as noted above with school, friends, and community workers assisting). However, families may not have wanted what they didn't know and offering new services may have presented new possibilities. This may have accounted for differences in families' views about integrated services at TFD sites compared to families' views in communities without integrated services.

Another illustration of families learning about new possibilities through TFD came from a survey question about the importance of various types of services asked in both early (2003) and full implementation (2005) surveys.

The most dramatic change over time across project sites was the increase in the importance of part-time child care. In 2003, 23% of families had ranked it among the most important services, but by 2005 that percentage had increased to 57%. Coincidentally, the sites had worked over the same period to "market" and make available a range of flexible childcare options. This was partly in response to families asking for more flexibility in scheduling of all services, but it was also partly a part of the "universal" mindset of the program developers—that all families, not just working families, have a need for occasional child care, to attend to family crises, for respite, etc.

Family Knowledge Building

The concept of knowledge building is relatively new in the area of education (Scardamalia & Bereiter, 2003) and has to this point not been directly applied to family involvement. This chapter has introduced the idea of "family knowledge building" as a corollary to practitioner knowledge building through iterative reflection and program modification. In this case, hearing what families wanted in early childhood services meant that families became part of the knowledge-building enterprise along with early childhood service professionals and with the research team. The process of knowledge building implies that individual members of a knowledge-building community contribute to and benefit from the "shared knowledge" that results. Ideas are strengthened when more views are added, theories revised, and practice is moved forward. By hearing what families wanted in the context of early childhood professionals' program goals, ideas were improved, programs were modified, and services became more integrated. Thus families themselves were contributors to and recipients of the new knowledge and programs that were designed to meet their needs.

LESSONS LEARNED AND RECOMMENDATIONS FOR PRACTICE

In this chapter we have argued that early childhood services for children and/or families should ask families what they want as one basis for developing and improving programs. Efforts to systematically and continually hear from families, including collection of regular narratives or data such as intake goals or preference polling for program features, can benefit children, families, programs, and communities; however, such efforts appear to be uncommon. Some attempts have been made in the area of special needs (Summers et al., 2001), but rarely in universal or preventative early childhood services.

This chapter brings together findings on multiple strategies that individual practitioners and organizations can pursue to build respectful engagement between families and early childhood services. They all emphasize the importance of hearing from families about their goals as part of designing and delivering needed and responsive services. Building upon this, five findings are noteworthy.

1. *Listen for difference.* The most general strategy that practitioners can adopt is listening for difference. Families have different needs and goals in accessing early childhood services. For example, parents are most often concerned with their children's social development and readiness but they also have goals for themselves, ranging from being part of a group to becoming a better parent. They also differ in how they want to be involved in their children's services. Volunteering and committee work aren't for everyone. Families' needs and goals may vary across different language groups and different neighborhoods, but the greatest differences are among individuals.

2. *Use multiple tools for systematic monitoring and collecting family input.* The most important concrete step in hearing from parents is systematic monitoring and collection of parental input from all parents. General communication and governance roles for some parents are not enough. Multiple tools can be used, such as intake and tracking systems, focus groups, surveys, and family–practitioner interviews with two-way exchange, to help ensure that all parents are heard from. High client satisfaction does not mean services are high quality or are doing all they can or meeting all families' needs; parents can indicate both high satisfaction and, with probing, point to areas that fall short. Families want to be heard from on a range of topics, from the design of services, how they want to be involved, the nature of curriculum, to individual child needs. Not every parent will want input on every topic, but every parent has something important to say.

3. *Share professional knowledge with families.* An important strategy in respectful and balanced communication is sharing what professionals know. For example, families may not want what they don't know. Balanced against open listening to families' goals should be efforts to build parents' capacity to understand the choices they have and what they should look for in early childhood services. If parents know "learning" as children being drilled while sitting in rows, will they necessarily understand the learning opportunities that structured play provides to young children? If parents don't know the dimensions of quality that define beneficial programs, how will they choose, or advocate for, improved services? If parents know services as traditionally separate kindergarten, child care, and parenting pro-

grams, will they see value in new options including integrated service arrangements that provide more seamless experiences for children and parents? Concrete strategies include educating parents about staff efforts to monitor and improve program quality and illustrating the value of structured play in building children's learning.

4. *Devise local action strategies.* Services can use information from community groups and individual families to build knowledge about how to improve. If staff have the time and tools and the collective aim of serving families better, they can devise local action strategies to meet the collective goals of parents and their organizations. They can monitor the results of their actions and revise them where appropriate. Effective communities of practice focus on the results and build respectful, satisfying relationships among the professionals and families they serve. At their best, communities of practice can become open to ideas and inputs from all stakeholders.

5. *Integrate and coordinate services.* Integration and coordination of traditionally separate early childhood services provide more opportunities to hear from parents and gives them choices to help meet their goals in a broader service array. The greater range of choices and more points of contact in the community through integrated service organizations also make for more effective outreach. Outreach is the first step in "hearing from parents."

CONCLUSION

Families increasingly see early childhood programs as preparing their children for school. This is not limited to academic learning and includes adaptation to the peer culture, the routines, and, for immigrant families, may include language and mainstream culture. For themselves, families want good care for their children when they work or attend school, and for all families, they want "community," including congenial interactions with other adults who have interests in children. Efforts to engage families in respectful ways are a foundation for these family, child, and professional communities. Respectful engagement includes hearing from families on their goals and, in return, sharing professional knowledge. Communities of practice can help professionals build knowledge about what parents want, devise responsive plans, and monitor results.

Beyond these general approaches to improving practice, we believe effectively engaging parents in early childhood services is a major first step in building their capacity for lifelong home–school–service community relationships (Patel & Corter, 2008). When school and early childhood services are linked, the capacity building for relationships is amplified. By removing the stigma associated with isolated, targeted preschool programs and providing a universal, family-friendly platform for accessing a variety of services, the "integrated" approach is a promising way of supporting the increasing diversity of today's societies.

ACKNOWLEDGMENTS

We are grateful to all family participants who contributed data to our research, with special thanks to Peter Varmuza and Joseph Lee of the City of Toronto Children's Services Division who contributed intake and tracking data. We would also like to acknowledge the contributions of other members of the Toronto First Duty Research Team—Jane Bertrand, Theresa Griffin, Donald McKay, Palmina Ioannone, Allia Karim, and Tomoko Arimura—as well as the administrative support of Christine Davidson in the Laidlaw Centre, Institute of Child Study. Funding support for the research on Toronto First Duty was provided by the Atkinson Charitable Foundation, the City of Toronto, and the Government of Canada's Social Development Partnerships Program. The opinions and interpretations in this publication are those of the research team and do not necessarily reflect those of the funders.

NOTE

1. By "parent" we mean the adult(s) who deal with services such as the parent, stepparent, guardian, grandparent, etc. We generally use the term "family" as a more inclusive term, but occasionally use the term "parent" for clarity in reporting research results or common usage in the literature (e.g., "parent involvement").

REFERENCES

Anderson-Parsons, B. (1997). Using a systems-change approach to building communities. St. Louis, MO: The Danforth Foundation.
Bernhard, J., Lefebvre, M. L., Kilbride, K. M. Chud, G., & Lange, R. (1998). Troubled relationships in early childhood education: Parent–teacher interactions in ethnoculturally diverse child care settings. *Early Education and Development, 9*(1), 5–28.
Bettler, R. F. (2001). Parents' goals and children's early cognitive development. *Dissertation Abstracts International.* (UMI No. 3015241)
Bettler, R. F., & Burns, B. (2003). *Research digest: Enhancing parental involvement through goal-based interventions.* Cambridge, MA: Harvard Family Research Project.

Bhering, E. (2002). Teachers' and parents' perceptions of parent involvement in Brazilian early years and primary education. *International Journal of Early Years Education, 10*(3), 227–241.

Cairney, T. H., & Munsie, L. (1995). Parent participation in literacy learning. *The Reading Teacher, 48*(5), 392–403.

Castro, D., Bryant, D., Peisner-Feinberg, E., & Skinner, M. (2004). Parent involvement in Head Start programs: The role of parent, teacher and classroom characteristics. *Early Childhood Research Quarterly, 19*, 413–430.

Ceci, S., & Papierno, P. (2005). The rhetoric and reality of gap closing. *American Psychologist, 60*, 149–160.

Corter, C., Bertrand, J., Pelletier, J., Griffin, T., McKay, D., Patel, S., et al. (2006). *Phase 1 Summary Report: Evidence-based understanding of integrated foundations for early childhood* (Toronto First Duty Phase 1 Final Report: Evidence-based understanding of integrated foundations for early childhood). Retrieved January 1, 2007, from http://www.toronto.ca/firstduty/TFD_Summary_Report_June06.pdf

Corter, C., Harris, P., & Pelletier, J. (1998). *Parent participation in elementary schools: The role of school councils in development and diversity.* Transfer Grant Report to the Ministry of Education and Training of Ontario.

Corter, C., & Park, N. (Eds.). (1993). *What makes exemplary kindergarten programs effective?* Toronto: Ontario Ministry of Education and Training.

Corter, C., Patel, S., Pelletier, J., & Bertrand, J. (in press). The Early Development Instrument as an evaluation and improvement tool for school-based, integrated services for young children and parents: the Toronto First Duty Project. *Early Education and Development.*

Corter, C., & Pelletier, J. (2005). Parent and community involvement in schools: Policy panacea or pandemic? In N. Bascia, A. Cumming, A. Datnow, K. Leithwood, & D. Livingstone (Eds.), *International handbook of educational policy* (pp. 295–327). Dordrecht, The Netherlands: Kluwer.

Cryer, D., Tietze, W., & Wessels, H. (2002). Parents' perceptions of their children's child care: a cross-national comparison. *Early Childhood Research Quarterly, 17*, 259–277.

Darling, N., & Steinberg, L. (1993). Parenting style as context: An integrative model. *Psychological Bulletin, 113*, 487–496.

Desimone, L., Payne, B., Fedoravicius, N., Henrich, C. C., & Finn-Stevenson, M. (2004). Comprehensive school reform: An implementation study of preschool programs in elementary schools. *Elementary School Journal, 104*(5), 369–389.

Dix, T. (1992). Parenting on behalf of the child: Empathic goals in the regulation of responsive parenting. In I. E. Sigel, A. V. McGillicuddy-DeLisi, & J. J. Goodnow (Eds.), *Parental belief systems: The psychological consequences for children* (2nd ed., pp. 319–346). Hillsdale, NJ: Erlbaum.

Epstein, J. L., & Salinas, K. C. (1993). *School and family partnerships: Surveys and summaries.* Baltimore: Center on Families, Communities, Schools, and Children's Learning and Center for Research on Effective Schooling for Disadvantaged Students, John Hopkins University.

Finn-Stevenson, M., Desimone, L., & Chung, A. (1998). Linking child care and support services with the school: Pilot evaluation of the school of the 21st century. *Children and Youth Services Review, 20*(3), 177–205.

Ho Sui-Chu, E., & Willms, J. D. (1996). Effects of parental involvement on eighth grade achievement. *Sociology of Education, 69*, 126–141.

Kagan, S. (1999). A5: Redefining 21st Century Early Care and Education. *Young Children, 54*(6), 2–3.

Kunkel, D., Smith, S., Suding, P., & Biely, E. (2006). Informative or not? Media coverage of child social policy issues. In A. Ben-Arieh & R. Goerge (Eds.), *Indicators of children's well-being* (pp. 173–191). Amsterdam: Springer.

Mattingly, D., Prislin, R., McKenzie, S. L., Rodriguez, J. L., & Kayzar, B. (2002). Evaluating evaluations: The case of parent involvement programs. *Review of Educational Research, 72*, 549–576.

National Association for the Educaiton of Young Children. (2004). *NAEYC Accreditation Readiness Survey.* Retrieved September 1, 2007, from http://www.naeyc.org/accreditation/pdf/

Organization for Economic Cooperation and Development. (1997). *Parents as partners in schooling.* Paris: Organization for Economic Cooperation and Development, Centre for Educational Research and Innovation.

Parker, K., & Leithwood, K. (2000). School councils' influence on school and classroom practice. *Peabody Journal of Education, 75*(4), 37–65.

Patel, S. (2004). *Parents, service integration and engagement in early childhood.* Unpublished master's thesis, University of Toronto, Toronto, Ontario, Canada.

Patel, S., & Corter, C. (2005, April). *Parents, preschool services and engagement with schools.* Poster session presented at the biennial meeting of the Society for Research in Child Development, Atlanta, GA.

Patel, S., & Corter, C. (2008). *Building capacity for parent involvement through school-based preschool services.* Manuscript submitted for publication.

Pelletier, J., & Brent, J. (2002). Parent participation in children' school readiness: The effects of parental self-efficacy, cultural diversity and teacher strategies. *International Journal of Early Childhood, 34*(1), 45–60.

Pelletier, J., & Corter, C. (2005). Design, implementation and outcomes of a school readiness program for diverse families. *School Community Journal, 15*, 89–116.

Pelletier, J., & Corter, C. (2006). Integration, innovation, and evaluation in school-based early childhood services. In B. Spodek & O. Sarracho (Eds.), *Handbook of research on the education of young children* (pp. 477–496). Mahwah, NJ: Erlbaum.

Pelletier, J., Reeve, R., & Halewood, C. (2006). Young children's knowledge building and literacy development through Knowledge Forum. *Early Education and Development, 17*(3), 323–346.

Pervin, L. A. (1989). Goal concepts in personality and social psychology: A historical introduction. In L. A. Pervin (Ed.), *Goal concepts in personality and social psychology* (pp. 1–17). Hillsdale, NJ: Erlbaum.

Pushor, D. (2007, January). *Parent engagement: Creating a shared world.* Invited paper presented at the Ontario Education Research Symposium, Toronto.

Scardamalia, M., & Bereiter, C. (2003). Beyond brainstorming: Sustained creative work with ideas. *Education Canada, 43*, 4–7.

Seitsinger, R. M., & Zera, D. A. (2002). The demise of parent involvement in school governance. *Journal of School Leadership, 12*, 340–367.

Sheldon, S. B. (2003). Linking school-family-community partnerships in urban elementary schools to student achievement on state tests. *Urban Review, 35*(2), 149–165.

Snyder, W. M., Wenger, E., & Briggs, X. D. S. (2004). Communities of practice in government: Leveraging knowledge for performance. *The Public Manager*, pp. 17–21.

Souto-Manning, M., & Lee, K. (2005). "In the beginning I thought it was all play": Parents' perceptions of the Project Approach in a second grade classroom. *School Community Journal, 15*(2), 7–20.

Stiles, A.S. (2005). Parenting needs, goals, and strategies of adolescent mothers. *MCN: American Journal of Maternal Child Nursing, 30*(5), 327–333.

Summers, J., Steeples, T., Peterson, C., Naig, L., McBride, S., Wall, S., et al. (2001). Policy and management supports for effective service integration in Early Head Start and Part C Programs. *Topics in Early Childhood Special Education, 21*(1), 16–30.

Wenger, E. (2000). Communities of practice and social learning systems. *Organization Articles*, 225–246.

Wenger, E. (2001). *Communities of practice: Learning as a social system.* Retrieved April 9, 2003, from http://www.co-i-l.com/coil/knowledge-garden/cop/lss.shtml

Wenger, E. (2004). Knowledge management as a doughnut: Shaping your knowledge strategy through communities of practice. *Ivey Business Journal*, pp. 1–8.

CHAPTER 7

BREAKING NEW GROUND

The Evolution of the Community School Concept in One City

Judy Harris Helm and Douglas P. Clark

At the new school, preschoolers and parents with infants and toddlers climbed down from the bus and were greeted by teachers. The children carefully followed pathways of colored tiles to their village classrooms. Some parents took their toddlers to the sibling care room before proceeding to their adult education and GED classes in the community classroom. Other parents went directly to the parent resource center to make books for their preschoolers and to learn about reading to children. In the school's health center, the nurse practitioner treated a child with an earache while another parent awaited a physical for work. It is 1993 and the first community school in Peoria, Illinois, the Valeska Hinton Early Childhood Education Center, opened for a typical day.

Promising Practices for Partnering with Families in the Early Years, pages 125–145
Copyright © 2008 by Information Age Publishing
All rights of reproduction in any form reserved.

INTRODUCTION

The Valeska Hinton Early Childhood Education Center is a comprehensive community early childhood center that was state of the art in the early 1990s and exemplified the collaborative community school model. It pioneered and still enables delivery of comprehensive family-centered early childhood services within a community school. In this chapter we consider the Valeska Hinton model as it was introduced in 1993 and still exists today. We go on to compare that model with plans emerging in 2007 for two new schools in the same school district. We highlight developments in national awareness and public policy pertaining to early childhood education that have precipitated important changes in the community school as interpreted in the Valeska Hinton early childhood program model and the model for two new schools being planned in 2007. We examine in greater detail how one facet of the community center related to the early childhood years (family, friend, and neighbor child care) might work using a new and more collaborative framework, and we conclude with our observation about how the new school model is truly breaking new ground.

VALESKA HINTON EARLY CHILDHOOD
EDUCATION CENTER, 1993

The Valeska Hinton Center is a community early childhood school in Peoria, Illinois. Opened in 1993, it was at that time a breakthrough comprehensive, full-day, year-round program for children ages 3–6. The center employed a three-member administrative team: a principal, a professional development coordinator, and a family liaison who oversaw community collaboration and parent events. Many program and design innovations have been attributed to the Valeska Hinton center. It is organized as four minischools, or villages of five classrooms each. Children enter and remain in the same village for 4 years. Children continue with one teaching team in a village when they are 3 and 4 years old, then with another teaching team within the same village when they are 5 and 6 years old.

The construction of Valeska Hinton, a Peoria public school, resulted from a 3-year planning and collaboration process involving the local school district, the city building commission, area businesses, the local community college, universities, and other early childhood programs in the city. Planning partners included Head Start, the YMCA, the Urban League, and other child care centers. Valeska Hinton was conceptualized as an intervention program primarily serving economically disadvantaged children and their families. Both the facility and program were designed as a way to coordinate services and education for young children, particularly those with low-income families, which comprised three-quarters of the school's enrollment.

Prior to the opening of Valeska Hinton, numerous programs and services existed for families of young children in Peoria. Although these offerings—which included Head Start and other public and private programs—enrolled many children, significantly more were not being served, putting them at greater risk for school failure (Lyman, 2000). When an urban renewal project opened the opportunity for a new facility to replace the old building, the district superintendent assembled a 15-member advisory committee that convened for over 2 years to develop the basic design of the new school (Helm, 1993b). This committee, chaired by the superintendent himself, studied relevant research, reviewed several school models, debated curriculum issues, and developed a vision for a "prototype community process to provide the best start for all its young, urban children" (Helm, 1993a, p. 57). As shown in Figure 7.1, the resulting school plan was depicted as a wheel with the school as the hub and spokes extending

Figure 7.1   Valeska Hinton shown as the primary coordinator of comprehensive early childhood services.

outward to connect with a broad array of community services ranging from adult education services to child care.

Building on the long-standing tradition in early childhood programs of reaching out to other agencies and organizations, the Valeska Hinton concept brought a public school into the spotlight as the centerpiece of collaboration and coordination. The school attracted a great deal of immediate interest and national attention. It quickly gained recognition as a model program, powerfully evidenced by over 17,000 visitors coming to observe the school in its first year of operation. The Valeska Hinton success story has been the subject of several research projects, books, and video media (Illinois STARnet, 1995; National Association for the Education of Young Children, North Central Regional Educational Laboratory [NCREL], 1996; Ward, 1996). Many components of this model have been replicated in numerous sites across the United States. Without question, Valeska Hinton is a school that broke paradigms and changed the thinking about what schools could and should do to serve young children, families, and the community.

BREAKING PARADIGMS

A New Task Force

The Valeska Hinton Early Childhood Education Center succeeded because of extensive community involvement in the design process. To realize the vision for Valeska Hinton, the original 15-person advisory committee was expanded to a 60-person task force comprised of community stakeholders and school district personnel. The task force operated as six working groups, each focused on a distinct aspect of the planning: (1) curriculum, (2) school climate and organization, (3) staffing and professional development, (4) student assessment and program evaluation, (5) student selection, and (6) working with families.

Consultants worked with these groups to present research and information on best practices and the decisions made by the working groups focused on how to overcome the many restrictive paradigms that influenced what people thought about public schools. Beginning with the first task force meetings, a high priority was placed on maximizing the involvement of families in the life of the center and in their children's education. From the task force's recommendations emerged an administrative model for the center, which entailed a three-person leadership team, including a family–community liaison responsible for facilitating parent involvement.

The workgroups shared specific considerations regarding values and beliefs about effectively working with families.

Valeska Hinton's Reconceptualized Model

As defined by the original advisory committee, a primary focus of the school's conceptual design emphasized that "the school will function as a family center with GED, adult basic education classes and parenting classes provided on site or through referral, networking and collaborative agreements with other agencies" (Helm, 1993b, p. 6). A second vital aspect of the conceptual design indicated that "parents will be integral participants in the planning and operation of the school" (p. 7). There was a strong commitment that the "school and teachers must include parents as equal partners"; an understanding, as Lyman (2000) points out, "many educators neither have nor practice" (p. 45). Once Valeska Hinton was erected, a parent advisory board was established and a variety of village and all-school social events were planned in an ongoing effort to further bond families with the center staff and each other. These examples, and others like them, evidenced the center's standing among a growing number of schools that were "redefining parent involvement" (Lyman, 2000).

Over a 7-month period, the workgroups identified goals and created detailed plans to pursue them. The emphases on these and other identified goals, plans, and teacher attributes led to program modifications that enabled the transformation from old to new paradigms as presented in Table 7.1. The establishment of these goals precipitated measures to identify the essential knowledge, skills, and dispositions that each staff member should possess to attain them. These parameters became the criteria for staff selection. For example, among the specific desirable characteristics related to working with children and families were general friendliness, belief in the ability of all children to achieve high expectations, and the capacity to work with children and families with diverse cultural backgrounds. Certain tasks, built into the employment interviewing process, provided additional insights about job applicants' attributes related to these staffing parameters.

As the center hired staff and the degree of their knowledge, skills, and beliefs became better known, it used this information to plan initial staff training. A significant part of the training prior to the opening of the school focused on the development of cross-cultural competency. During these training activities staff identified their own cultural backgrounds and experiences and learned how these might influence their relationships with children and families with diverse cultural backgrounds.

TABLE 7.2 Paradigms from Valeska Hinton Center, 1993

Old Paradigm	New Paradigm	Program modifications
School is for children.	School is for families and school is the place where everyone goes to learn. The family is considered the child's first and most important teacher and parents are seen as partners in the child's education. School is a place for teachers to continue to learn and grow.	The school building was designed to provide a parent area for parent classes, sibling care, small-group activities, and networking. A professional development center and training room were added.
Everybody is the same.	Teachers understand and work with children and families from various cultural backgrounds. Teachers and children value and respect diversity and feel comfortable with a variety of people.	Training was provided that focused on teachers recognizing their own culture and learning about the culture of others. Teacher training is ongoing.
Changing homes means changing schools.	The school and village are a stable, secure environment for children and families.	Children are transported to the school no matter where they move in the city of Peoria. Logistics plans were developed to accommodate 20 buses and to board children in developmentally appropriate ways.
The school year is 9 months.	The school year is all year. Summer vacation is broken into smaller vacations throughout the year to decrease loss of learning in the summer.	A modified 45-15 day model enables the center's children to be off when holidays and vacations occurred in the other schools in the district. Contracts, food services, maintenance schedules, transportation services, and other working agreements were modified.
The school day is 6 hours long.	The school day is from 8:45 AM to 3:15 PM but the school is open from 6:30 AM to 5:30 PM for families who need child care before and after school.	Agreements were developed with funding agencies for the school to receive funds for providing child care. A staff was hired and trained to provide the care.
The school is not responsible for physical care of the child.	School is an access point for other services that families need to provide a healthy start for their young child. Physical development of the child is an important part of the school goals.	Agreements were developed with health service organizations to provide on-site health care for children and families. Two nutritious meals and a snack are served each day. Naps and teeth brushing are part of the daily schedule.

NEW CONSIDERATIONS OF EARLY LEARNING AT THE DAWN OF THE NEW MILLENNIUM

National Trends

In the years that have passed since the 1993 construction of the Valeska Hinton center, findings from a broad base of research on child development and early learning, increased national awareness about the importance of the early years, and policy changes at both federal and state levels all have prompted new ways of thinking about how to best serve children, families, and communities. These approaches recognize the importance of quality early care and learning experiences. They urge close working relationships among school systems, Head Start programs, child care providers, and community services agencies.

In the wake of the relative absence of national policies on child care and early childhood education, federal legislation emerging during the 1990s and the beginning of the 21st century has had a profound impact on access and availability of early childhood education and care for thousands of families across the United States. As America approached the second millennium, convictions about motherhood and family life that had shaped early childhood policy during most of the preceding century were giving way in the debates over welfare reform (Lombardi, 2003; Michel, 1999). Consensus was eventually reached for national policy that would bring publicly supported parents into the paid labor force and "end welfare as we know it" (Clinton Foundation, n.d.). The Personal Responsibility and Work Opportunity Reconciliation Act, often referred to as welfare-to-work legislation, transformed the U.S. welfare system by replacing legal entitlement to cash assistance under the previous welfare program with the Temporary Assistance for Needy Families (TANF) block grant. The new law requires low-income parents with children ages 3 months and older to be employed within 2 years of claiming welfare payments and sets a 5-year lifetime limit for any individual receiving benefits (Kamerman & Gatenio, 2003).

Amid the changing political, societal, and economic climate anticipated from enacted welfare reform law, the Child Care Bureau was established in 1995 within the U.S. Department of Health and Human Services as the lead agency overseeing federal child care programs. The Bureau plays several important roles, most prominently the administration of the Child Care and Development Fund (CCDF), which administers $4.8 billion to support improvements in the availability, access, and quality of child care for low-income families (U.S. Department of Health and Human Services, 2004). As the Child Care Bureau's first chief executive, Joan Lombardi (2003) noted that by placing child care in a children's agency, and outside a purely welfare or social-welfare orientation, a "new direction was set" (p. 46). It envisioned child care as a two-generation program: both a service to promote healthy child development as well as a work support for family self-sufficiency.

Heightened Public Awareness

During the years that welfare reform laws took shape, a wave of interest in brain research and early education emerged and rapidly gained momentum. For instance, the Carnegie Corporation of New York (1994) published *Starting Points*, a report on the importance of the first 3 years of a child's life, which raised awareness about parenting, children's development, and the quality of early childhood experiences. In popular literature, a special issue of *Newsweek* magazine (Begley, 1997) was devoted to the early years of life. Actor and filmmaker Rob Reiner lent his celebrity as spokesman for the *I Am Your Child* campaign (Parents' Action for Children, 2005), intended to spread the word about the link between healthy early brain development and positive child outcomes. Shonkoff and Phillips's (2000) *From Neurons to Neighborhoods,* prominent in the academic literature, reported among its findings that all children were born "ready to learn"; "early environments matter"; and "society is changing and the needs of young children are not being addressed" (p. 4).

The release of published research and heightened public awareness highlighted the critical importance of the early years—whether spent at home or in nonresidential child care—to children's overall development. These occurrences drew attention to the positive influence of quality child care on children in both formal school-based programs and informal home-based child care settings (Cost, Quality, and Child Outcomes Study Team, 1995; Galinsky, Howes, Kontos, & Shinn, 1994). They confronted existing paradigms by challenging the dichotomous *either/or* mindset pertaining to matters of child care and those of preschool education. In Lombardi's (2003) words, "improving child care and reforming education...appeared to be 'two sides of the same coin'" (p. 45).

Good Start, Grow Smart

In 2002, Congress enacted the *No Child Left Behind Act (NCLB)* with bipartisan backing. NCLB has been celebrated by some and criticized by others for its dramatic impact on elementary and secondary schools. A lesser known provision of NCLB called for a $75 million emphasis on literacy in early childhood programs (Lombardi, 2003). As a result, the federal government instituted the *Good Start, Grow Smart* early childhood initiative to help states and local communities strengthen early learning for young children. *Good Start, Grow Smart* emphasizes coordination of child care services and collaboration among stakeholders to develop a high-quality early learning system ensuring that all children will enter kindergarten prepared to succeed in school (Child Care Bureau, 2004).

Illinois Initiatives

In Illinois, the notion of coordinating early childhood services among stakeholders is exemplified by the *Preschool for All* initiative, which was signed into law in the summer of 2006 (Illinois State Board of Education [ISBE], 2006). Underwritten by federal and state block grant dollars, *Preschool for All* represents the expansion of the publicly funded state prekindergarten program that began 20 years earlier to serve families with "children who are at risk of academic failure because of their home and community environment" (ISBE, 2004, p. 1). Although the high-need population remained a priority during the program buildup period, *Preschool for All* established Illinois as the first state with plans to make preschool available for all 3 and 4-year-olds (State of Illinois, 2006).

Illinois is among the states at the forefront of the national prekindergarten movement, a movement that while young is growing at a swift pace. A report by the National Institute for Early Education Research (Barnett, Hustedt, Robin, & Schulman, 2006) indicates that the number of prekindergarten programs in the United States has virtually doubled since 1985. During the 2004–2005 school year, 38 states served nearly 1 million children. More growth is expected, suggesting that state prekindergarten enrollment will exceed federal Head Start enrollment at all ages in the very near future. As this expansion continues, it is anticipated that more states will follow Illinois' lead by increasing their public prekindergarten offerings to serve families and the community through universal access for all preschool-age children, not just those who are deemed at risk.

Research outcomes, increased public awareness, and sweeping legislation have added to a new school design team's collective understanding about how schools for young children can be more effective. In particular, the momentum of the national prekindergarten movement suggests fresh opportunities for new schools—such as those being planned in Peoria—to rewrite the meaning of comprehensive early childhood services.

PEORIA'S NEW CITY PARK SCHOOLS

Planners of the 2010 New City Park Schools of Peoria are taking into account these developments on the national scene, as well as the lessons learned from real experiences in Peoria. In 2006, the school district initiated a new school design endeavor, and once again a visionary superintendent has selected a community school model for this high-poverty area. The design team is embracing a contemporary model that situates the new school among a network of partner peers who share the work of coordinating and administering comprehensive early childhood services.

School as Coordinator

Heifets and Blank (2004) argue that partnerships among a wide range of stakeholders—social agencies, family support initiatives, faith-based institutions, and other community groups—are at the core of community schools. These partnerships are deliberate and provide the supports and opportunities that are important to all stakeholders: students, families, and the surrounding community as demonstrated by the Valeska Hinton model. Throughout the first decade and a half of its operation, the school has existed as the center for coordination, much like the model Hiatt-Michael (2003) describes as a school "whose meaning and purpose move beyond academics to child and family well-being" (p. 3).

Although the Valeska Hinton services delivery model is cast in the spirit of collaboration, in practice the school functions mainly as the primary *coordinator* of each component of the comprehensive portfolio of services for children and families. And over the years of its existence, *coordinating* has become highly labor intensive, not only for the Valeska Hinton school staff, but also for the entire school district. While the school's primary mission is comprehensive early childhood education and services, the administration of the center requires the skills, time, and resources needed for management of a large community center. Turnover among the school administrative team members has been high: Over the span of time that Valeska Hinton has been open, the average length of stay for a principal or professional development coordinator is less than 3 years.

School as Collaborative Partner

Plans for the new schools entail a concept similar to the one Dryfoos (2003) describes as a full-service community school, where a community agency "establishes a peer relationship with a school system by taking on the responsibility for some of the workings of the school" (p. 35). Her contentions about community partners assuming responsibility for the coordination of some services represent a subtle but important paradigmatic shift: One that transcends the notion of the community school acting as central coordinating agent to a new model that views the school as partner and peer.

New Paradigm Shifts

The new schools—named City Park Schools because they will be built in park-like settings to provide nature experiences—will be organized and operate differently than the Valeska Hinton Center, breaking new ground in many important ways. The new designs are informed by the evidence from research and take into account the growing national emphasis on school achievement and the emergence of multiple public funding streams (child care subsidies, along with state prekindergarten and federal Head Start grants) to support early childhood education and the experiences of the community.

The most noticeable differences between the new community schools and Valeska Hinton are programmatic design approaches that expand the age range of children and students being served. Where Valeska Hinton was designed as an early childhood education center serving children from ages 3–6, the new schools will provide for families with children from birth through eighth grade. Although the schools will serve an expanded age range, the plan calls for a student population not to exceed 500 children. Among the advantages found in the research on the benefits of smaller schools (Clinchy, 2000; Howley, 1994; Wasley et al., 2000; Wasley & Lear, 2001), families will find it easier to identify with the school staff.

Continuity of active, engaged teaching at all age levels will require project-based learning and space for engaged learning experiences in each classroom. A welcoming attitude toward families will also be emphasized to keep them involved in their children's education over the trajectory of their entire school experience. Once the new schools are built, specific strategies to accomplish this goal will be developed jointly by teachers and parents.

The community has learned that it is not enough to just give children a good start. Observations over time at Valeska Hinton have shown that children's smooth transition into the primary and middle school experiences are critical for school success. Therefore, the vision for the new schools includes provisions for the development of a clear plan for each child's growth and individual achievement throughout their years within the school. Each child will be carefully monitored and special support provided during transitions from grade to grade This emphasis on the individual child and monitoring of achievement allows teachers to incorporate developmentally effective practices that are consistent with the spirit of the NCLB law. It will be carried out through staff development and professional learning communities that are focused on knowledge and skills needed by teachers to support children's learning. Methods of meaningful, continuous updating will be developed with each family: for some, they may have informal conferences; for others, it might be systematic phone conferences or emails.

From School Hub to Partnerships

Easily overlooked by the casual observer, but likely the most significant of the differences between the new and original school designs, is the reconceptualization of the services delivery model. The Valeska Hinton school, functioning as the *hub of the wheel*, was housed in a single self-contained building that is owned, supervised, and maintained by the school district. In the New City Park Schools, community organizations will provide experiences for the children and families within the school, as well as for senior citizens, young professionals, teens, and other residents of the neighborhoods near the school buildings.

Community organizations will also assume more responsibility for the programming and the funding of those experiences. In this way the school succeeds by bringing together many partners to offer a range of supports and opportunities to children, youth, families, and members of the community before, during, and after school, 7 days a week. Stakeholders in this model—individuals, schools, businesses, and public and private organizations—become partners in addressing community needs. The school is one of many partners that provide academic, recreation, health, social service, and work-preparation programs for people of all ages within a neighborhood (Parsons, 2003). Often referred to as *learning centers*, these schools emphasize lifelong learning, community involvement, and efficient use of resources. As is the case for the New City Park Schools services delivery model shown in Figure 7.2, a learning center is often organized as a campus system within which multiple program components are contained. This figure depicts a sharp contrast to the model shown in Figure 7.1 with the school as the hub. In the new model, each agency is a separate entity with proximity providing easy accessibility and collaboration, at the same time enabling independence of each organization and reducing the administrative and budgetary burden on the school.

In Peoria, it is likely that some of these program components will not be contained within the school building itself or owned by the school district. For example, the health clinic may be connected by a walkway. Each new school will be individually designed based on the needs of the proximal neighborhood. The land on which the school is erected will be maintained by the local park district, which will provide not only landscaping, but also basketball courts, playing fields, hiking trails, and classes as identified in

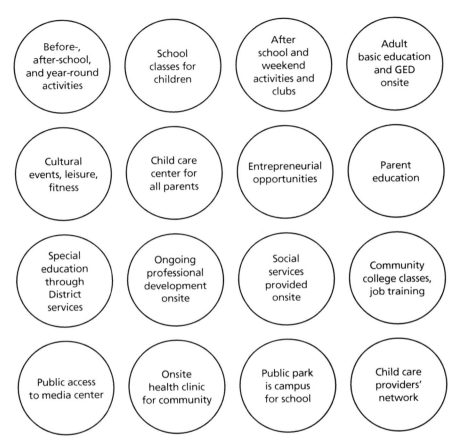

Figure 7.2 New City Park Schools services delivery model with potential programming components to be incorporated based on neighborhood needs.

the needs assessment, which will take place in each neighborhood. In exchange, the school will house a park district office within the building plus locker rooms adjacent to the gym area and accessible during weekends for park district events and activities that will be staffed by park district.

Arrangements such as these demonstrate a new paradigm, one which highlights a shift away from school-directed events to neighborhood events that are accessible and meaningful to the whole community: all ages, all economic levels, and not just those in need or deemed at risk. In keeping with this conceptual framework, planners of the new schools are also contemplating the establishment of a small business center that could stimulate entrepreneurial and economic opportunity by inviting members of the local business community onto the school campus and providing opportunities for students to observe and participate in authentic business experiences.

Plans such as those just described view the *school* within the community school as one of several vital components of a community redevelopment plan. Preliminary architectural renderings of the New City Park Schools for Peoria indicate how this new thinking influences design, as over 40% of the space is designated for flexible use that will enable community utilization of the facility at times of the day and week when it is not being used by the school. The intentionality of designating spaces that enable partner organizations to assume responsibility for supervision and programming represents a significant paradigmatic shift in school design.

And finally, the new design departs from the traditional model of the teacher–parent dyad where all experiences are related to school intervention or the school relating directly to the parent or the family. By reducing the role of the school as intervener, the new paradigm fosters community building. This new approach builds a community by providing networks, spaces, and support. Emphasizing school as a place or catalyst for the partnering organizations rather than the school as the coordinating hub, community members develop their own relationships, which in the long run directly impact children's achievement in school. One example of how relationships might be fostered to support families and enhance children's early care and education in a community school is the family, friend, and neighbor child care provider network being considered for Peoria's New City Park Schools.

NEW PARADIGMS IN PRACTICE: CHILD CARE PROVIDER RESOURCE CENTER

Family, Friend, and Neighbor Care

To meet the demands of employment or job training in the wake of national welfare reform legislation, a substantial proportion of families require child care services that can accommodate nontraditional or nonroutine schedules such as overnight, weekend, or split-shift work arrangements. When unable to provide care for their children during these hours, families often rely on relatives, friends, and neighbors. This is a typical pattern of care for families in the areas of the planned New City Park Schools. Family, friend, and neighbor child care providers have a formidable potential influence on the early development and later school achievement of the children in their care, yet they are difficult to reach with current information on caregiving or resources which would make their work more effective (Krajec, Bloom, Talan, & Clark, 2001). New data about the needs and interests of these providers has prompted the New City Park Schools design team to consider innovative ways to better serve them in the neighborhoods where the new schools will be located.

In 2005, federal and state monies underwrote a large proportion of the cost of child care services for over 1.7 million children from income-eligible families. Nationally, 25% of these children were cared for in settings in which a government-issued license to operate is not required, those the U.S. Child Care Bureau defines as "legally operating without regulation." While this figure accurately suggests that about one in four American children served by state-administered subsidies is cared for in family, friend, or neighbor child care settings, in many geographic areas the percentages are quite higher. In Illinois, for instance, the use of family, friend, and neighbor child care accounts for over half (51%) of all children receiving services via the state's subsidized child care program, a level that on average impacts more than 40,000 children each month (U.S. Child Care Bureau, 2007).

The Connections Survey

In September 2005, the *Connections* survey was conducted with Illinois license-exempt child care providers who had received payments for their services through the subsidy program (Clark, 2007). Administered by telephone, the survey solicited family, friend, and neighbor providers' responses to questions about the human and institutional sources they believed could provide them with reliable information about early childhood education and care.

Findings revealed that Illinois family, friend, and neighbor child care providers view educators and educational institutions as the sources they would trust most for information about early childhood education and care. This is particularly the case when providers are seeking information related to their roles in helping the children in their care to enter kindergarten prepared to succeed in school. While it is not surprising that schools, teachers, and other educators were the most common sources indicated by survey respondents as best-suited to give advice on matters related to school readiness, typical responses included *local teacher, local school*, or *a teacher I know*. In each of these cases, providers' answers indicated not just that they would seek advice from educators generally, but that in particular they would look to those involved with their local school.

Connecting Family, Friend, and Neighbor Care Providers with Schools

One of the goals of community schools is to "connect services from the community with the children and families served by the school" (Hiatt-Michael,

2003, p. 2). In considering how to provide the best possible start to all children before their kindergarten years—not just those in formal early care and learning settings—it is fitting to incorporate into the plans for the new schools a means for reaching out to family, friend, and neighbor child care providers in the local community. Findings from the *Connections* research suggested that placing a child care provider resource center on the premises of a community school is a practice with real promise. Such a center could be used as a place for child care providers to seek early childhood information from a trusted source, for access to printed materials and online resources, and for nurturing a community of child care practitioners.

Locating a provider resource center within a school translates the aims of national and state policy to local scale in keeping with *Good Start, Grow Smart*, which is intended to support children's school readiness through the coordination of activities and collaboration among federal, state, and local child care and early childhood development programs (Child Care Bureau, 2004). Those interviewed for the *Connections* study indicated their respect for local teachers and school personnel as sources they would trust for information related to early childhood education and care. They also indicated high levels of interest in learning more about how they can help the children in their care attain state school readiness goals. Using the school as a resource site is especially appropriate because it can provide an inviting venue for family, friend, and neighbor child care providers to benefit from the coordination of resources and collaboration by key stakeholders intended to ensure that all children enter kindergarten prepared to succeed in school.

Vision for a Family, Friend, and Neighbor Provider Resource Center

The *Connections* research calls for the piloting of a provider resource center that could be operated by a certified early childhood teacher or other personnel on staff at the new schools with current early childhood teaching credentials. A site-based resource center would serve as a place for family, friend, and neighbor providers within its proximity to access credible information, materials, and technical assistance. In many ways, this approach mirrors that of erecting public libraries within the walls of public schools for joint use by students and the community-at-large (Wisconsin Department of Public Instruction, 1998). In keeping with the flexible design approach adopted for use throughout the New City Park Schools planning initiative, dedicated space need not be designated for the child care provider resource center. Other spaces within the school campus, perhaps the library or sibling care area provided for adult education, might be utilized without further impingement on school resources.

Plans for the New City Park Schools include the availability of rolling carts for organizations and agencies from outside the school to use when occupying flexible space areas. These carts will be lockable and can house resources, notebook computers, materials for work, and organization files. A resource group for family, friend, and neighbor providers can meet within the school building, perhaps with a staff member from the local child care resource and referral agency to receive the support, training, and organizational skills needed on the school site. In this manner, the school building functions as a gateway for connecting providers with resources to inform their caregiving practices in light of state school readiness goals.

Establishing a physical space inside a local school building to support family, friend, and neighbor child caregivers addresses both the *high-touch* and the *high-tech* aspects associated with efforts to link providers with resources to enhance their caregiving practices. Besides face-to-face access to school personnel and informative materials, the provider resource center would also offer access to computers, help in learning basic computing skills, and training on the effective use of the Internet, which would expand its reach beyond the brick-and-mortar paradigm of merely locating a child care resource center on the school campus. The school-housed center would serve as an initial connecting point for family, friend, and neighbor providers to meet and to share knowledge and experiences with each other. The sharing of knowledge and common experiences furthers the cultivation of a community of practice among family, friend, and neighbor providers, a community with the potential to flourish simultaneously in the on-campus and online venues and spread out into the neighborhoods. In this way, the new paradigm of the community school as one part of a networked community, or campus, can be leveraged well beyond the walls of the school building. Once online, new possibilities—perhaps limitless ones—arise for connecting a community of family, friend, and neighbor child care providers across the city and linking it to the collective expertise of other early childhood practitioners regardless of their physical locations. Relationships that develop within these networks can continue to develop outside of the school and extend into and beyond the neighborhood without the school being an intermediary.

BREAKING NEW GROUND

The current state of planning for the new schools of Peoria is heavily influenced by significant changes that have occurred in early childhood research, state school policy, and in the beliefs about the role of the school in the community. In contrast with the Valeska Hinton Early Childhood Education Center designed in the early 1990s, the New City Park Schools will operate less as coordinator of comprehensive services and more as collaborator among a host of community partner peers.

The Valeska Hinton Center broke paradigms by providing for the physical care of the child bringing health services into the school. The new schools will provide connection to these and other meaningful services that will support the unique needs and goals of the local community. Whereas the Valeska Hinton Center embodies the school as a location for all the community to come to learn, the new schools envision the community as a center for learning providing learning opportunities for all, including those in the school. Whereas the Valeska Hinton Center was designed to provide a good start and focused on the early years, the new schools see all the years as important and a good start as the first step along that pathway.

As plans for the new school are crystallizing, so emerges a new wave of thinking about what schools can do to serve young children, families, and their communities. Similar to the shift away from prekindergarten provided by the public for children at risk toward a new system with universal access to prekindergarten for all children, the new community school in Peoria will be for all its citizens, not just those who are considered to be in greatest need.

This evolving model of the community learning center is easy to imagine for neighborhoods where children and families face poverty and health needs. It is, however, just as relevant for communities where children and families face fewer and lesser hardships. For example, in an upscale suburb in Ohio there is a child care center where the program director has installed a commercial coffee machine so families can pick up their morning cup of coffee after they drop off their children and before they begin their commute. She says as the parents wait for their coffee to brew, it provides an opportunity for them to connect with each other, to observe children's work displayed on the walls and see what is going on at the center, to talk about their children, to bypass the coffee shop on their morning commute, and to begin their day with a smile.

The placement of one coffee machine in a child care center lobby appears to be cultivating a sense of community in an Ohio suburb, which begs new questions. Would the model embodied in the New City Park Schools design concept be equally effective in addressing needs important to parents and families in other community settings? Could the school as a neighborhood learning center usher in a rich sense of the community by embracing the growing diversity of families and cultures everywhere? If so, this is indeed the most compelling breakthrough of all, a paradigm shift that transcends the others. For schools to be successful places for young children, schools must be places for the community and *all its people*. This message is clear to those planning the new schools of Peoria and their revelation shows promise for building effective schools in all communities throughout Illinois and beyond.

ACKNOWLEDGMENTS

The authors wish to acknowledge the work of the school design committee, Superintendent Kenneth Hinton, and the staff and administration of Peoria Public Schools for their support and willingness to share their design process. In addition, we wish to acknowledge the Child Care Bureau of the U.S. Department of Human Services, Administration for Children and Families for its financial support to underwrite the Making the Most of Connections research study.

REFERENCES

Barnett, W., Hustedt, J., Robin, K., & Schulman, K. (2006). *The state of preschool: 2005 state preschool yearbook.* New Brunswick, NJ: National Institute for Early Education Research.

Begley, S. (1997, Spring/Summer). How to build a baby's brain. In *Your child from birth to 3, Newsweek* [Special issue], pp. 28–32.

Carnegie Corporation. (1994). *Starting points: Meeting the needs of our youngest children.* New York: Carnegie Corporation.

Child Care Bureau. (2004). *A guide to Good Start, Grow Smart in child care.* Washington, DC: U.S. Department of Human Services Administration for Children and Families.

Child Care Bureau. (2007). *FFY 2005 CCDF data tables.* Retrieved September 19, 2007, from http://www.acf.hhs.gov/programs/ccb/data/ccdf_data/05acf800/list.htm

Clark, D. (2007). Making the most of connections: Illinois license-exempt child care providers' use of information about early childhood education and care. (Doctoral dissertation, Pepperdine University, 2006). *Dissertation Abstracts International, 67,* 10A. (UMI No. 3238903)

Clinchy, E. (Ed.). (2000). *Creating new schools: How small schools are changing American education.* New York: Teachers College Press.

Clinton Foundation. (n.d.). *Press briefing by Mike McCurry: May 21, 1996.* Retrieved April 8, 2005, from http://www.clintonfoundation.org/legacy/052196-press-briefing-by-mike-mccurry.htm

Cost, Quality, and Child Outcomes Study Team. (1995). *Cost, quality, and child outcomes in child care centers, executive summary.* Denver: University of Colorado, Economics Department.

144 ▪ J. H. HELM and D. P. CLARK

Dryfoos, J. G. (2003). A full-service community school. In D. Hiatt-Michael (Ed.), *Promising practices to connect schools with the community* (pp. 35–47). Greenwich, CT: Information Age.

Galinsky, E., Howes, C., Kontos, S., & Shinn, M. (1994). *The study of children in family child care and relative care: Highlights of findings.* New York: Families and Work Institute.

Heifets, O., & Blank, M. (2004, January/February). Community schools: Engaging parents and families. *Our Children.* Retrieved May 19, 2006, from http://www.communityschools.org/OurChildren.pdf

Helm, J. (1993b). History of the project. Unpublished manuscript. Peoria Public Schools.

Helm, J. (1993a). Community collaboration for an early childhood center. *Beckley-Cardy Quarterly, 6*(4), 57–59.

Hiatt-Michael, D. (Ed.). (2003). *Promising practices to connect schools with the community.* Greenwich, CT: Information Age.

Howley, C. (1994). *The academic effectiveness of small-scale schooling (an update).* ERIC Digest. Charleston, WV: ERIC Clearinghouse on Rural Education and Small Schools. (ERIC Document Reproduction Service No. ED 372 897)

Illinois STARnet (Producer). (1995 April 19). *Breaking paradigms: The Valeska Hinton Early Childhood Center* [Videotape]. (Available from STARnet Regions I & III, Center for Best Practices, Western Illinois University, Horrabin Hall 27, Macomb, IL 61455)

Illinois State Board of Education. (2004). *Illinois pre-kindergarten program for children at risk of academic failure: Fiscal year 2003 evaluation report.* Springfield: Illinois State Board of Education.

Illinois State Board of Education. (2006). *Preschool for All funding report: Fiscal year 2007.* Springfield: Illinois State Board of Education.

Kamerman, S., & Gatenio, S. (2003). Overview of the current policy context. In *Early childhood care and education in the USA* (pp. 1–30). Baltimore: Paul H. Brookes.

Krajec, V., Bloom, P., Talan, T., & Clark, D. (2001). *Who's caring for the kids? The status of the early childhood workforce in Illinois.* Wheeling, IL: Center for Early Childhood Leadership.

Lombardi, J. (2003). *Time to care: Redesigning child care to promote education, support families, and build communities.* Philadelphia: Temple University Press.

Lyman, (2000). *How do they know you care: The principal's challenge.* New York: Teachers College Press.

Michel, S. (1999). *Children's interests/mothers' rights: The shaping of America's child care policy.* New Haven, CT: Yale University Press.

National Association for the Education of Young Children, North Central Regional Educational Laboratory, Nebraska Department of Education Stark County Schools. (Producers). (1996). *Early childhood video library* [Videotape]. (Available from NAEYC, 1313 L Street, NW, Suite 500, Washington, DC 20005)

North Central Regional Educational Laboratory. (1999) Critical issue: *Organizing for effective programs and practices.* Retrieved January 17, 2006, from http://www.ncrel.org/sdrs/areas/issues/students/earlycld/ea100.htm

Parents' Action for Children. (2005). *History: I am your child.* Retrieved May 1, 2005, from http://www.parentsaction.org/about/history/http://www.nccic.org/pubs/definition-fcc.pdf

Parsons, S. R. (2003). *Journey into community: Looking inside the community learning center.* Larchmont, NY: Eye on Education, Inc.

Shonkoff, J., & Phillips, D. (Eds.). (2000). *From neurons to neighborhoods: The science of early childhood development.* Washington, DC: National Academy Press.

State of Illinois. (2006). *Gov. Blagojevich signs groundbreaking Preschool for All legislation.* Retrieved January 15, 2007, from http://www.illinois.gov/PressReleases/ShowPressRelease.cfm?SubjectID=2&RecNum=5108

U.S. Department of Health and Human Services. (2004). Notices. *Federal Register, 69*(81), 22811–22819.

Ward, C. (1996). *Recultivating Froebel's kindergarten for a post-modern society.* Unpublished doctoral dissertation, Southern Illinois University, Carbondale.

Wasley, P., Fine, M., Gladden, M., Holland, N., King, S., Mosak, E., et al. (2000). *Small schools: Great strides. A study of new small schools in Chicago.* New York: Bank Street College of Education.

Wasley, P., & Lear, R. (2001, March). Small schools, Real gains. *Educational Leadership, 58*(6), 22–27.

Wisconsin Department of Public Instruction. (1998). *Combined school and public libraries guidelines for decision making* (2nd ed.). Madison: Wisconsin Department of Public Instruction.

APPENDIX

RECOMMENDED RESOURCES BY CHAPTER

Introduction

Mary M. Cornish

Strategies for Working with Diverse Families

Gonzalez-Mena, J. (2007). *50 early childhood strategies for working and communicating with diverse families.* Upper Saddle River, NJ: Pearson Merrill Prentice Hall.

This user-friendly book presents 50 practical strategies for partnering with families to improving the quality of care and education of young children ages birth to 8. Each strategy is presented with a rationale followed by a variety of recommended approaches.

Family-Centered Programs

Keyser, J. (2006). *From parents to partners: Building a family-centered early childhood program.* St. Paul, MN: Redleaf Press.

Intended for teachers, caregivers, home-based child care providers, and family, friend, and neighbor care providers, the book presents a comprehensive set of approaches for promoting family-centered programs. It pro-

Promising Practices for Partnering with Families in the Early Years, pages 147–163
Copyright © 2008 by Information Age Publishing
All rights of reproduction in any form reserved.
147

vides a wide variety of tips, practical advice, vignettes, and sample dialogues. Reflection exercises are included throughout the book to support readers in connecting their "thinking, practice, and experience."

Teacher Preparation

National Institute on Early Childhood Development and Education. (2001). *New teacher for a new century: The future of early childhood professional preparation.* Jessup, MD: U.S. Department f Education.

This publication examines and depicts what constitutes high-quality teacher preparation at the baccalaureate level. One chapter, among the many useful chapters, focuses on preparing early childhood professionals to work with families. It explores the issues, ideals, realities, and barriers associated with this work. Promising developments in the field and lessons from model personnel preparation programs are shared.

Home–School–Community Linkages

Regional Educational Laboratories' Early Childhood Collaboration Network. (2002). *Continuity in early childhood: A framework for home, school, and community linkages.* Jessup, MD: U.S. Department of Education, Office of Education Research and Improvement.

This publication guides the development of linkages among services for children birth through age 8 and their families. It presents eight elements of continuity with a rationale, effective practices, and specific indicators for each. *Families as Partners* is one of the eight elements. Practices associated with partnering with families are infused throughout many of the other elements. Helpful forms are included to serve as tools for program self-assessment. The document provides a comprehensive approach for establishing home, school, and community partnerships.

Chapter 1
Family Involvement Promotes Success for Young Children:
A Review of Recent Research

Heather Weiss, Margaret Caspe, and M. Elena Lopez

**Early Childhood and Family Involvement Resources from
Harvard Family Research Project**

Join the Family Involvement Network of Educators (FINE)
The Family Involvement Network of Educators (FINE) is a national network of over 7,500 people who are interested in promoting strong partner-

ships between children's educators, their families, and their communities. There is no cost to become a FINE member. Once you join, you will receive our monthly announcements via email of current ideas in family involvement. You will also be alerted to new additions to the FINE 2ebsite such as *Taking a Closer Look: A Guide to Online Resources on Family Involvement.* This document contains Web links to research, information, programs, and tools from over 100 national organizations.

To join FINE, visit www.gse.harvard.edu/hfrp/projects/fine/joinfine.html

To access the Resource Guide, go to www.gse.harvard.edu/hfrp/projects/fine/resources/guide/guide.html

The Family Involvement Storybook Corner

This section of the Harvard Family Research Project (HFRP) website is a unique source for information on using children's storybooks with family involvement themes to engage families in their children's education and encourage family–school–community partnerships, all while supporting literacy.

www.gse.harvard.edu/hfrp/projects/fine/resources/storybook/index.html

Bibliography on Family Involvement in Early Childhood

This bibliography, compiled by the Harvard Family Research Project, highlights family involvement research literature related to early childhood.

www.gse.harvard.edu/hfrp/projects/fine/resources/bibliography/ece.html

Evaluation Exchange: Evaluating Family Involvement Programs

This issue of *The Evaluation Exchange* addresses the challenges of evaluating family programs, such as the need for conceptual clarity, methodological rigor, accountability, and contextual responsiveness.

www.gse.harvard.edu/hfrp/eval/issue28/index.html

Getting Parents "Ready" for Kindergarten: The Role of Early Childhood Education

Holly Kreider of HFRP suggests that family involvement in young children's education may contribute to a smooth transition to elementary school for children and prepare parents for later involvement in their children's learning.

http://www.gse.harvard.edu/hfrp/projects/fine/resources/research/kreider.html

The Transition to Kindergarten: A Review of Current Research and
Promising Practices to Involve Families
Marielle Bohan-Baker and Priscilla Little of HFRP look at the transition
to kindergarten and its importance to school success, focusing on promising transition practices and the role that schools might play in the implementation of these practices.
http://www.gse.harvard.edu/hfrp/projects/fine/resources/research/
bohan.html

Chapter 2
Learning from the Field of Early Intervention about
Partnering with Families

Pamela J. Winton, Mary Jane Brotherson,
and Jean Ann Summers

Resources for Learning from the Field of Early Intervention
about Partnering with Families

Organizations and Centers

Beach Center on Disability
http://www.beachcenter.org
This website provides information about current and past work by Beach
Center investigators as well as related products. Both full research articles
and shortened "research highlights" are available on topics including family involvement, collaboration, cultural diversity, self-determination, participatory action research, disability policy, and much more. The section called
"Real Stories and Tips" features contributions from families and service
providers. The site also includes discussion boards on various topics, links
to parent organizations, and a quarterly newsletter.

Division for Early Childhood (DEC)
http://www.dec-sped.org
The Division for Early Childhood (DEC) is one of 17 divisions of the
Council for Exceptional Children (CEC)—the largest international professional organization dedicated to improving educational outcomes. DEC is
especially for individuals who work with or on behalf of children with special needs, birth through age 8, and their families. DEC offers a variety of
publications as well as the *Journal of Early Intervention* and *Young Exceptional*
Children.

National Association for the Education of Young Children (NAEYC)

http://www.naeyc.org

The National Association for the Education of Young Children (NAEYC) is dedicated to improving the well-being of all young children, with particular focus on the quality of educational and developmental services for all children from birth through age 8. Membership is open to all individuals who share a desire to serve and act on behalf of the needs and rights of all young children.

Parents as Teachers (PAT)

http://www.parentsasteachers.org

Email: info@parentsasteachers.org

Parents as Teachers is the overarching program philosophy of providing parents with child development knowledge and parenting support. Their vision is that all children will learn, grow, and develop to realize their full potential. The mission is to provide the information, support, and encouragement parents need to help their children develop optimally during the crucial early years of life.

Parent Training (PTI)

http://www.taalliance.org

Email: alliance@taalliance.org

Each state is home to at least one parent center. Parent centers serve families of children with all disabilities: physical, cognitive, emotional, and learning. They help families obtain appropriate education and services for their children with disabilities; work to improve education results for all children; train and inform parents and professionals on a variety of topics; resolve problems between families and schools or other agencies; and connect children with disabilities to community resources that address their needs. This website offers links to research, publications, translated material, and many other resources.

Parent to Parent

http://www.p2pusa.org

Key to supporting parents in linking them to other parents who have had similar experiences. Parent to Parent-USA (P2P-USA) is a national nonprofit organization committed to ensuring access and quality in Parent to Parent support for families nationally with children who have a special health care need or disability. This website offers research, technical assistance, FAQs, and other beneficial links to related sites.

Zero to Three

http://www.zerotothree.org

ZERO TO THREE is a national nonprofit, multidisciplinary organization that supports the healthy development and well-being of infants, toddlers, and their families. They carry out that mission through a range of activities that inform, educate, and support the adults who influence and nurture very young children's lives. This website provides links to information and publications for infants and their caregivers.

Family Voices

http://www.familyvoices.org
Email: kidshealth@familyvoices.org
Family Voices is a national network of families, friends, professionals, and advocates who focus on health care services. The focus is on providing health care that is family centered, community based, comprehensive, coordinated, and culturally competent.

Family Village

http://www.familyvillage.wisc.edu
Email: familyvillage@waisman.wisc.edu
The comprehensive website provides extensive information for families of children with disabilities related to recreation and leisure, education, health, and daily living. They provide both print and electronic resources.

Culturally and Linguistically Appropriate Services (CLAS)

http://clas.uiuc.edu/aboutclas.html
The CLAS Institute identifies, evaluates, and promotes effective and appropriate early intervention practices and preschool practices that are sensitive and respectful to children and families from culturally and linguistically diverse backgrounds.

Through this website, Janet Gonzalez-Mena has videos that provide a new way to help people in child care integrate culturally responsive caregiving with developmentally appropriate practices. Those videos go far beyond on-site observations. You see a multiethnic group of early childhood professionals who are struggling over what quality child care for children ages 0–6 means in a culturally sensitive context that values diversity. Suspending judgment about right and wrong, the primary goal is to show diverse perspectives—and to help people in child care open up communications and create powerful, new connections with each other, with parents, and with the children. Viewers uncover preconceived notions, are exposed to other viewpoints, and think through conflict resolution, all in a safe context.

Video #1—Diversity, Independence, and Individuality
Video #2—Diversity: Contrasting Perspectives
Video #3—Diversity and Communication
Video #4—Diversity and Conflict Management

Our-Kids: Devoted to Raising Special Kids with Special Needs
  http://www.our-kids.org/
  Our-Kids is a "family" of parents, caregivers, and others who are working with children with physical and/or mental disabilities and delays. In the website, they discuss their children's accomplishments and defeats, knowing that the audience includes others who know what they are going through. They can also provide some idea of how others address specific problems/concerns with feeding, learning, schools, medical resources, techniques, and equipment, as well as describing the problems to friends and family or just coping.

Print Resources

Building Connections with Families by Using Family Involvement Storybooks
  Read about ideas for using family involvement storybooks in this article from *Young Children*, a journal of the National Association for the Education of Young Children (NAEYC). The authors describe five ways for teachers to use family involvement storybooks in their classrooms. The article also includes a vignette about the impact of sharing a family involvement storybook in one third-grade class. You can access the article at http://www.gse.harvard.edu/hfrp/projects/fine/resources/storybook/reference.html. For more resources on using storybooks to promote family involvement, visit http://www.gse.harvard.edu/hfrp/projects/fine/resources/storybook/index.html

Complementary Learning
  Using family involvement storybooks is just one way to put into action the Harvard Family Research Project's "complementary learning" approach to closing the achievement gap. Complementary learning is a comprehensive model that fosters partnerships between families, schools, and other non-school supports. You can learn more about complementary learning at http://www.gse.harvard.edu/hfrp/projects/complementary-learning.html

Communities of Practice: A New Approach to Solving Complex Educational Problems
  This guideline, published by the National Association of State Directors of Special Education (NASDSE) as part of the IDEA Partnership, outlines a model for building Communities of Practice (CoP). This approach for engaging stakeholder groups in solving complex and persistent problems has been used in many different formats. However, this manual provides an overview of the approach that the IDEA Partnership has developed for special education, with a particular focus on state agency personnel. Contact NASDE at www.nasdse.org for more information.

Position Statements

Division for Early Childhood (DEC) Position Statement on Responsiveness to Family Cultures, Values and Language

> http://www.dec-sped.org/pdf/positionpapers/Position Family Resp.pdf

This document summarizes DEC's position on responsiveness to family cultures, values, and language. The position paper discusses characteristics of responsive organizations, providing useful suggestions for practitioners working with families.

Responding to Linguistic and Cultural Diversity: Recommendations for Effective Early Childhood Education (a position statement of the National Association for the Education of Young Children/NAEYC)

> http://www.naeyc.org/about/positions/pdf/psdiv98.pdf (English)
> http://www.naeyc.org/about/positions/pdf/psdisp98.pdf (Spanish)

For the optimal development and learning of all children, educators must accept the legitimacy of children's home language, respect and value the home culture, and encourage the active involvement and support of all families, including extended and nontraditional family units. This position statement underscores NAEYC's commitment to these principles.

Chapter 3
Family Partnerships in Early Childhood Programs: Don't Forget Fathers/Men

Brent A. McBride, Wm. Justin Dyer, and Thomas R. Rane

Resources for Supporting Father Involvement

Print Resources

Fagan, J., & Palm, G. (2004). *Fathers and early childhood programs.* Clifton Park, NY: Delmar.

This book provides helpful insights and a detailed overview on how early childhood programs can create initiatives to encourage men to become more involved in their classrooms and with their children.

Pleck, J. H., & Masciadrelli, B. P. (2004). Paternal involvement by U.S. resident fathers: Levels, sources, and consequences. In M. E. Lamb (Ed.), *The role of the father in child development* (4th ed., pp. 222–271). New York: Wiley.

This chapter provides an in-depth analysis of the research literature examining the antecedents and consequences of father involvement.

The Fathering Indicators Framework

Gadsden, V., Fagan, J., Ray, A., & Davis, J.E. (2001). *The Fathering Indicators Framework: A tool for quantitative and qualitative analysis.* Available at the National Center on Fathers and Families website: http://www.ncof.gse.upenn.edu

This document provides an introductory overview of the Fathering Indicators Framework and how it can be used as a self-assessment tool for identifying strengths and limitations in the ways in which early childhood programs reach out to fathers.

Chapter 4
Easing the Transition: Family Support Programs and Early School Success

Billie J. Enz, Michelle Rhodes, and Marilyn LaCount

Websites of Featured Programs

AVANCE. www.avance.org

Bright Beginnings. http://www.cms.k12.nc.us/programs/brightbeginnings/brightbeginnings.asp

Educare. http://www.educareomaha.com/news.asp

Even Start. http://www.ed.gov/programs/evenstartformula/index.html

Leaps and Bounds. www.asu.edu/leapsandbounds

New Directions Institute for Infant Brain Development. www.newdirectionsinstitute.org.

Parent University. http://www.mpsaz.org/parentu/index.htm

Schools of the 21st Century. http://www.yale.edu/bushcenter/21C/history.html

SPARK. http://www.wkkf.org/default.aspx?tabid=75&CID=168&NID=61&LanguageID=0

Chapter 5
Home-Based Care Plays an Important Role in Meeting Family Needs

Lori Connor-Tadros and Dawn Ramsburg

Resources for Home-Based Care Play an Important Role in Meeting Families' Needs

Organizations

Child Care Bureau (CCB)
http://www.acf.hhs.gov/programs/ccb

The Child Care Bureau, Administration for Children and Families, U.S. Department of Health and Human Services, administers federal funds to states, territories, and tribes to assist low-income families in accessing quality child care for children when the parents work or participate in education or training.

Council for Professional Recognition
http://www.cdacouncil.org

The Council for Professional Recognition works to meet the growing need for qualified early care and education professionals who care for children from birth through age 5 in Head Start and prekindergarten programs, child care centers, family child care homes, and as home visitors. The Council promotes the Child Development Associate (CDA), a national credentialing program that focuses on the skills of early care and education professionals. The CDA is designed to provide performance-based training, assessment, and credentialing of early care and education staff.

Early Head Start National Resource Center (EHS NRC)
http://www.ehsnrc.org

EHS NRC was created in 1995 by the Office of Head Start (formerly the Head Start Bureau), Administration for Children and Families, U.S. Department of Health and Human Services. The EHS NRC links the Early Head Start and the Head Start community through opportunities in coordination with the Office of Head Start's Early Childhood Learning and Knowledge Center. EHS NRC also creates, collects, and disseminates information relevant to comprehensive early childhood programs. In addition, it provides professional development opportunities for the Early Head Start and Head Start community through face-to-face meetings and state-of-the-art distance learning experiences.

Early Head Start (EHS) is a federally funded community-based program for low-income families with infants and toddlers and pregnant women. Its mission is to promote healthy prenatal outcomes for pregnant women, enhance the development of very young children, and promote healthy family functioning.

Family Strengthening Policy Center (FSPC)

http://www.nassembly.org/fspc/index.html

The Family Strengthening Policy Center (FSPC) is an initiative of the National Assembly, an 80-year-old alliance of leading national nonprofit health and human service organizations. Funded by the Annie E. Casey Foundation, the FSPC is part of the Foundation's Neighborhood Transformation/Family Development and Making Connections initiatives. The Casey initiatives are intended to improve outcomes for children and families living in low-income, marginalized communities by advancing and promoting family-strengthening practice.

Harvard Family Research Project (HFRP)

http://www.gse.harvard.edu/hfrp

Email: hfrp@gse.harvard.edu

HFRP strives to increase the effectiveness of public and private organizations and communities as they promote child development, student achievement, healthy family functioning, and community development. In its relationships with national, state, and local partners, HFRP fosters a sustainable learning process—one that relies on the collection, analysis, synthesis, and application of information to guide problem solving and decision making. HFRP was founded in 1983 at the Harvard Graduate School of Education (HGSE) Institute for a Child Care Continuum

National Association of Child Care Resource and Referral Agencies (NACCRRA)

http://www.naccrra.org/about/program.php?Page=1

For information on Child Care Aware, see http://www.childcareaware.org/en/

NACCRRA works with more than 800 state and local Child Care Resource and Referral agencies to ensure that families in every local community have access to high-quality, affordable child care. NACCRRA leads projects that increase the quality and availability of child care, offer comprehensive training to child care professionals, undertake groundbreaking research, and advocate child care policies that positively impact the lives of children and families. NACCRA hosts *Child Care Aware,* a national toll-free child care consumer telephone hotline and website funded by the Child Care Bureau, links families to their local, community-based child care resource and referral program, and consumer education materials to ensure families have access to accurate, useful information about finding child care.

National Resource Center for Health and Safety in Child Care and Early Education (NRC)

http://nrc.uchsc.edu/

NRC's primary mission is to promote health and safety in out-of-home child care settings throughout the nation. *Caring for Our Children: National Health and Safety Performance Standards Guidelines for Out-of-Home Child Care Programs, Second Edition* (2002) is available on the NRC website. The licensure regulations from the 50 states, the District of Columbia, Puerto Rico, and the Virgin Islands are also available on this website. The NRC is funded by the Maternal and Child Health Bureau, U.S. Department of Health and Human Services.

Office of Head Start (OHS)

http://www.acf.hhs.gov/programs/hsb/

Head Start is a nationwide early childhood program for preschool children in low-income families. It is designed to provide comprehensive services in preparation for public school. It has served children and their families since 1965. Head Start is a Federal program that is designed to foster the healthy development of children from low-income families. In general, Head Start serves children whose family income is at or below the Federal Poverty Income Guidelines. However, Head Start programs may serve a limited number of children from families above this income limit. To find a local Head Start program to contact in your area, use the online national Head Start Locator Tool at http://eclkc.ohs.acf.hhs.gov/hslc/HeadStart-Offices.

Smart Start Initiative

www.ncsmartstart.org

Email: yhhuntley@ncsmartstart.org

Smart Start is North Carolina's early childhood initiative designed to ensure that young children enter school healthy and ready to succeed. It is a public–private initiative that provides early education funding to all of the state's 100 counties. Smart Start funds are administered at the local level through local nonprofit organizations called Local Partnerships. Smart Start's National Technical Assistance Center (NTAC) provides assistance to states and localities that are working to ensure that every child arrives at school healthy and ready to succeed.

Sparking Connections

Families and Work Institute (FWI)

www.familiesandwork.org/sparking/home.htm

Sparking Connections is a demonstration and evaluation project of FWI. It is a three-phase, 4-year national initiative to demonstrate and evaluate strategies to support FFN caregivers through partnerships with retailers and other nontraditional partners. The Sparking Connections National Consortium—a 2-year evaluation and demonstration project (Phase II)—began in December 2003 following the publication of FWI's Sparking Connections report.

Additional Resources

Enhanced Home Visiting Project Pilot Project (EHVP)

Early Head Start National Resource Center @ ZERO TO THREE
www.ehsnrc.org/highlights/EHVP.htm

EHVP provides Early Head Start programs an opportunity to assess and address the needs of FFN caregivers who provide services for children enrolled in Early Head Start. There are 24 participating Early Head Start and Migrant Head Start infant and toddler programs serving children in home-based settings where the children's parents are working and the children are in the care of relatives or neighbors. These programs received funding to develop and implement an enhanced home visiting program to serve children in FFN care settings. The home visiting models recognize that children's nonparental caregivers must have the knowledge, training, and skills necessary to help children develop their highest potential.

Institute for a Child Care Continuum

Bank Street College of Education
www.bankstreet.edu/ICCC/
Email: tporter@bnkst.edu

The Institute supports the quality care for children across the child care continuum, including the quality of FFN care. It initiated the National Alliance for Family, Friend and Neighbor Child Care (NAFFNCC), a work group that helps influence FFN policies, enhance providers' access to services, and increase the awareness of the role FFN providers play in the child care system. For additional information, call Toni Porter at (212) 961-3420.

Institute for Youth, Education, and Families (YEF Institute)

National League of Cities
http://www.nlc.org/ASSETS/2F54313C904C4CF1890EFD8AAFBCE68D/IYEF_FFN_Care.pdf
Email: holsclaw@nlc.org

The YEF Institute is partnering with the United Way of America on a FFN care initiative. Recognizing that most young children are in family, friend, and neighbor (FFN) care settings during the day when their parents are working, the initiative aims to strengthen the capacity of city, United Way, community group, and other local leaders to support and conduct effective outreach to FFN care providers.

National Association for Family Child Care (NAFCC)

http://www.nafcc.org

Email: nafcc@nafcc.org

NAFCC is a national membership organization of family day care providers and local and State family day care associations. It sponsors an annual national conference and an accreditation program for family day care providers. NAFCC has about 7,500 members and is governed by an executive committee and 10 regional representatives. NAFCC is focusing its efforts on supporting family child care associations and promoting quality through accreditation.

National Alliance for Family, Friend and Neighbor Child Care (NAFFNCC)

Bank Street College

http://www.bnkst.edu/naffncc

NAFFNCC is a work group of individuals and organizations that share a common interest in family, friend, and neighbor child care. It consists of a diverse group of practitioners, researchers, and policymakers who are at the forefront of work in this field. NAFFNCC aims to influence policies for family, friend, and neighbor care; enhance caregivers' access to services; and increase awareness of the role that family, friend, and neighbor child care plays in the child care system.

National Association for Regulatory Administration (NARA)

http://www.nara-licensing.org

NARA is a membership organization with a vision of consumer protection through prevention. It represents all human care licensing, including child care, child welfare, adult day care, adult residential and assisted living care, and program licensing for services related to mental illness, developmental disabilities, and abuse of drugs and alcohol. NARA members include human service regulatory professionals, human service providers, university faculty, independent researchers and consultants, allied professions from the health, safety, and legal disciplines, and consumers.

National Center for Children in Poverty (NCCP)

Joseph L. Mailman School of Public Health of Columbia University

www.nccp.org

The mission of NCCP is to identify and promote strategies that prevent young children from experiencing poverty in the United States, and improve the lives of the millions of children younger than age 6 who are growing up poor. NCCP has published materials that relate to FFN care.

National Child Care Information Center (NCCIC)

http://nccic.acf.hhs.gov

Email: info@nccic.org

NCCIC, a service of the Child Care Bureau, Office of Family Assistance, is a national clearinghouse and technical assistance center that links parents, providers, policymakers, researchers, and the public to early care and education information. It has information on many topics, including information about licensing, quality rating systems, the Child Care and Development Fund, state-funded prekindergarten initiatives, family child care, and family, friend, and neighbor care.

Child Care and Early Education Research Connections

www.researchconnections.org

Email: contact@researchconnections.org

Research Connections offers a comprehensive, up-to-date, and easily searchable online collection of more than 11,000 resources from the many disciplines related to child care and early education. Interactive tools allow users to refine their searches, download full text documents, build customized tables on state policies, compare state demographics, and analyze research data online. Publications include research briefs on *Measuring Quality in Family, Friend, and Neighbor Care* (http://www.researchconnections.org/location/ccrca12033) and *Assessing Initiatives for Family, Friend, and Neighbor Child Care* (http://www.researchconnections.org/location/ccrca11787). Also, a recent Review of Research summarizes literature on *Family Child Care in the United States* (http://www.researchconnections.org/location/ccrca12036).

Chapter 6
What Do Families Want? Understanding Their Goals for Early Childhood Services

Sejal Patel, Carl Corter, and Janette Pelletier

The First Duty Indicators of Change Tool

A general description of the Indicators of Change tool is available online (see http://www.toronto.ca/firstduty/indicators_oct2005.pdf). The tool describes progress toward service integration on a continuum of change that includes coexistence, coordination, collaboration, and integration as benchmarks. It presents levels of integration for five dimensions, including parent involvement. Incremental steps for improving family input are laid out for a number of subdimensions: family input into program decisions, family participation in programs, parenting capacity, and relationships with families.

Communities of Practice

Wenger, E. (2004). Knowledge management as a doughnut: Shaping your knowledge strategy through communities of practice. *Ivey Business Journal*, pp. 1–8.

This article describes how to facilitate knowledge-building through communities of practice. It defines the term and identifies three fundamental characteristics of communities of practice. It gives advice regarding how to form and engage in communities of practice.

Chapter 7
Breaking New Ground: The Evolution of the Community School Concept in One City

Judy Harris Helm and Douglas P. Clark

Academic Development Institute
http://www.adi.org

The Academic Development Institute (ADI) works with families, schools, and communities so that all children may become self-directed learners, avid readers, and responsible citizens, respecting themselves and those around them. Among its services, ADI administers the Center on Innovation and Improvement, publishes the *School Community Journal*, and partners with numerous family, school, and community supports across the United States. Among its many publications, ADI offers the resource *Standards Start at Home—A Parent Guide to Early Learning.*

Best Practices, Inc.
http://www.bestpracticesinc.net

Best Practices is a consulting and training company for early childhood and elementary schools (preschool, prekindergarten, kindergarten, and primary grades) begun by Dr. Judy Harris Helm. Best Practices provides onsite observations; guided self-assessment of active, engaged learning; training in specific skills such as play intervention or project approach; designing preschool activities; early literacy; and implementation of authentic assessment systems.

Child Care and Early Education Research Connections
http://www.childcareresearch.org

Child Care and Early Education Research Connections promotes high-quality research in child care and early education and the use of that research in policymaking. The Research Connections website offers research and data resources for researchers, policymakers, practitioners, and others. Research Connections is a partnership among the National Center for Children in Poverty (NCCP) at the Mailman School of Public Health, Columbia University; the Inter-university Consortium for Political and Social Research (ICPSR) at the Institute for Social Research, the University of Michigan;

THE LIBRARY
NEW COLLEGE
SWINDON
WITHDRAWN

and the Child Care Bureau, Office of Family Assistance, and the Office for Planning, Research and Evaluation (OPRE) in the Administration for Children and Families of the U.S. Department of Health and Human Services.

Gateways to Opportunity

http://www.ilgateways.com

Gateways to Opportunity is a statewide network designed to support peer networking, career guidance, education, training resources, and credentialing for early care and education professionals in Illinois. Gateways to Opportunity is specifically designed to meet the needs of early care and education professionals in Illinois who work in family child care center-based care; relative, friend, and neighbor care; early childhood special education; early intervention; public education; Head Start; and other early childhood programs and settings.

The McCormick Tribune Center for Early Childhood Leadership at National-Louis University

http://cecl.nl.edu

The McCormick Tribune Center for Early Childhood Leadership is dedicated to enhancing the management skills, professional orientation, and leadership capacity of early childhood administrators. The activities of the center encompass four areas: training, technical assistance, research, and public awareness. Center faculty Teri Talan and Paula Jorde Bloom developed the *Program Administration Scale* (PAS) as a tool for measuring the overall quality of administrative practices of early care and education programs. In conjunction with the 2007 launch of *Quality Counts*—the new quality rating system for family child care and center-based early care and education programs in Illinois—teams from the McCormick Tribune Center conduct all on-site assessments of classroom and program quality required for the star-rating system.

Pre-K Now

http://www.preknow.org

Pre-K Now collaborates with advocates and policymakers to lead a movement for high-quality, voluntary prekindergarten for all 3- and 4-year-olds. Pre-K Now advances prekindergarten programs for all children by providing financial and technical assistance to advocates for new and existing public prekindergarten programs and strengthening the capacity and skills of early childhood advocates and state leaders to secure policy changes and funding. Pre-K Now strives to educate and mobilize key sectors of the public and policymakers at the state and national level about the severity of the American school readiness problem and the potential that high-quality prekindergarten for all has for addressing the problem and boosting K–12 student achievement for all children.